Original title:

Memórias de uma Alma

Author - José Micard Teixeira

Translation - Ingrid Koehler Micard Teixeira

ISBN: 9798857136393

Memoirs of a Soul

José Micard Teixeira

To my children,

Yannick, Ingrid and Mel

I can't forget those who tell me they won't forget me. I still don't quite understand what the main reason is, but I'm beginning to believe it comes from my need to be remembered by some. I don't want to get addicted to memories, because they also remind me of the suffering side of much of what I've experienced. I guess I just want to feel that someone smiles when they remember who I was in their life. It makes me feel cozy. Peaceful. Almost like a dog or a cat nestled in the lap of the one who has chosen to protect it from cold and loneliness. For a brief instant that is worth a lifetime.

I like to carry your nakedness with me while I dress myself. I look at you without disturbing your sleep. I love to see you lying on the sheets pulled over your body. I smell your scent on my skin and smell myself smiling. I run my fingers through my hair and seem to feel your hands still clutched in them as we whispered words of desire and madness and made promises of life and death. I love the way we love each other body and soul. We think of nothing because there is nothing to think about. There is only a time that happens in less time than all the other time we have left. A time of our own. Only ours. As if it were the first of all. The one we will one day retrieve from our memories to remember a kiss. A groan. A touch of skin. A blindness where you continued to see everything, because in truth you could never forget anything.

Nothing is eternal. Everything that begins ends. In the same way that one day all of this began, in the same way all of this will one day end. I don't know when or in what way. I only know that nothing lasts forever. Eternity is just a concept we have created to better deal with the end of things and people we love and with the inevitability of death. Eternity has a certain duration. It is not up to the thinkers but to the scientists to determine when it will happen. It is up to us to know how to live this eternity in the best way possible. As long as it lasts. As long as it is worthwhile.

When I stick the needle into the least painful vein in my arm, I immediately feel an anger that I know exists only in my head. My body aches even more than the last few times. It feels torn into a thousand wounds joined together only to remind me of what I'd like to forget. Breathing hangs between before and what I hope to feel in a few seconds. Blood rushes fast to me and I scream against god in that measly space of time when I realise my human misery. I curse what led me so much to believe in what ultimately destroys me. At that moment, I feel like ripping out the needle and the life that kills me inside and out, get up and run until I die. Instead, I feel myself tumbling slowly over my right side, on a blanket that smells of rain and smoke. I cannot counteract the movement of my body that falls without strength. I know that in a moment I will forget everything. The pain. The suffering. The shame. The fear. The snot that runs from my nose and the tears I can no longer cry. I know I'm going where I wouldn't want to go anymore. If only it was death. If only it wouldn't hurt again. Slowly, I feel my lips twitch into a stupid, meaningless smile. The worst part is about to begin. The part where I start believing in happiness again, in love, in life. The part where I roll over on my arm and feel like hugging myself. But it lasts a little while. Too little. Just the instant of one more thought. Of an absence of something I never knew I wanted so much. The time for a squint before I stop feeling what matter I am made of or if my body has turned into something less than wind. A nothing without anything. An echo without a mountain. A void torn by a new pain, even more relentless than all the others. Obstinate. Even more pain. A pain that reminds me that I am still alive, despite the naive hope that I might finally be dead.

I have stopped seeing or foreseeing the end of every thing. I refuse to leave all the moments in which I live. They are mine and of those who are with me. I know I may sound inconsequential, but I want the future to be damned. I don't even know if I'm going to get there. I just know that I'm here, now, doing what I like to do, writing what I feel like writing without having to give justifications to anyone about the words I choose. That's what freedom is. It is stripping away. It is sensitivity. It's raising my head in front of those who want to make me stop smiling. It's not a thinking about what doesn't matter anymore. It is making love as if each time were the best of all times. It is to provoke what is stopped for lack of courage to change. It is to trust myself above all. Right now. In this instant.

Never later, because waiting for later is only for those who live without any word being able to define exactly what they so often fail to live.

If I only accept to live what makes sense to me now, I will live very little. There is so much more in life that has long since stopped making sense to me or that I have never found any. I want to live every moment, every stop, every feeling and emotion of everything and in everything. I toast some and all for what they make me feel and experience when I don't distance myself. There are no exceptions in anything that comes to me. Everything ends up gaining meaning from what it represents to me. Even what I have seen a thousand times. Even what I no longer want to see. Everything that comes to me has a meaning for me that I may not yet know. I no longer run away or hide from it. I may even be afraid. Even very afraid. But I have learnt that the meaning of things is often in what we insist on not wanting to see. Nor accept. Nor love.

I don't want a balanced life. A life made without uncertainty or unforeseen events becomes a life that is too predictable. Predictability is an invitation to flee from everything different. A life that is always the same kills without taking life. It is a suicide that seems to not exist, but that is always happening. Every second. At each choice of the same. With every desire for coherence and certainty. I haven't wished for a balanced life for a long time. I want adventure and unexpected passions. Trips scheduled from one day to the next. Madnesses that seem to have a life of their own. Parties at the house of people I've never seen and in places so hidden they don't appear on maps. Words cut at the root so they don't always say the same thing. Things done for the first time without losing the magic of when they are done for the last time. I want everything that never seems balanced. I want nothing that reminds me of the calmness of an ocean that I always need to feel in the middle of storms and islands in the sun.

I like people who live without shit, who don't get bored or waste time with stupidities without any importance, who forgive with their heart and don't cling to meaningless arguments, who uncomplicate what doesn't need to be complicated, who send to hell what doesn't deserve less than that, who say they love someone or something with the same honesty with which they state the opposite, who tell anyone who has betrayed or disrespected them to fuck off and give them no more chances so that there is no room for new lies and deceit, who do not draw conclusions without knowing the facts, who always listen to the other side, who do not give a damn about what is right and proper if they feel like doing it differently, who often make arrogant people swallow their stupidity with a well deserved figurative slap in the face, who do not follow fashions or dogmas, who sing in the street and in the shower, who undo whatever insists on stopping or deceiving them, who give a few corny compliments to those who ask for them, who think little and feel more and more, and above all who love with their whole heart, without half measures, because they realised long ago that life is not just something more or less given to them as a punishment for some fucked-up karma, but rather a great and passionate adventure that they set out to live even before they got here.

The hardest thing is to meet someone who looks at me and sees me. Most people only see in me what they want to see of myself. They can't look at me through my eyes. They are not able to feel me beyond what they decide to allow themselves to feel. They let me bring them only memories of what they least wish to remember. They look at me with their eyes and never more than with their eyes. They refuse to see beyond them. They are afraid to see what they are not prepared for. They believe their eyes are their truth. My truth is that I don't really like people who only see with their eyes. They don't see much of anything. They prefer to see only what blinds them. What they fail to see, even after opening their eyes.

I like people of science who keep a rabbit's foot in their pocket. I love people who never say goodbye or talk about what they don't have. I love those who insist on not dying before their time and live intensely until their last breath of life. I like all those who know how to live without internet or television while they are with me, those who open a book of poetry and read me a poem as if they had written it themselves. I love all those who have a connection with me that quiets both my loneliness and my desire to be alone. The truth is that I always have time for those who bring life into my life. For those who ask me for generous doses of who I am.

I need the fuss of my own company more and more. I am absolutely nobody without me. I love myself without needing to receive anything in return. I don't demand anything from myself beyond what I want to be. I don't need to do this or that to please myself. I accept myself as I am. Without taking away or putting away anything. When I don't like something about myself, I smile. Nothing solves my life better than a smile. Nothing transforms me more than a smile.

I don't want to sound unfair when I say that my parents didn't love me. They could not do so, because they did not love themselves. This truth is unquestionable. We can only give who we are. The love they showed for me was to the extent of what they knew about love. They knew very little. Yet they were caregivers. They took care of me. They made me grow to the extent of their fears and uncertainties. They disowned me of love and made me believe in who they told me I was. Even without words. Even without love. I grew up in a lifeboat without oars, lost in a sea of endless currents and successive shipwrecks. I swam as best I could and reached an island. I made it mine and kept it in my dreams. I made a different love grow on it. More mine. A love of more love. Almost without memories of the past. A love to the extent of who I became for myself. To the extent of what in my eyes never ceased to be mine.

There are times when you are not aware that time has passed and you with it. Each and every life has a moment that made all the difference. It's not several. It's just one. It's the one where you chose something stupid that you should have never chosen for yourself. From that instant on, your whole life turned upside down and nothing else could be the way it should have been. Years later, there was another moment. Just one. A moment when you could have changed everything again. A single one, no more than one. A single moment when, despite everything, you chose to continue in the same moment. You were afraid of being even more afraid and you stayed. You didn't dare. You died without even daring to live. You died because you didn't believe that changing the past might not be an impossibility.

Everything I make possible in my life paves the way for my ability to trust myself more and more. My path has fewer and fewer secrets. When I don't know, I give. When I don't understand, I listen. When I don't want to, I don't do it. Everything is simple when I don't complicate it. If I attract, it is mine. I need to accept it to change. This is the only way I can commit to myself. To my mission. To my piece of heaven down here.

Don't force me to be forced. I don't mind bleeding, but let it be from wounds of freedom. All obligation tears off parts of my skin and marks every corner of my soul with pain. I was not born to be forced to do anything. No one is born to be forced to anything. We are born to choose in freedom what our heart asks for. I have been living this way for a long time now. I no longer torture myself with obligations or efforts. I have become free by myself. To be obligated is an imprudence that each one allows. I have left that behind. I no longer live several lives in one. I live only one. The one which one day became my favourite. The one that allows me to rest and smile at the same time.

To be happy, all you have to do is stop being stupid. Unhappiness is stupidity. Only those who don't understand anything about life stay in it. One can easily become sad, but remaining unhappy is only for those who see suffering as the greatest talent for bringing others together. To stay in suffering too long is a real stupidity. The truth is that suffering exists only so that one can get out of it and understand how not to come back. You only learn after letting go of all the suffering. During, it only hurts. Nothing changes. Not even the pain. It is only when you decide to be happy that you start to let go of what never had anything to do with you. Everything that remains finally has our name on it. Our face. Our movement.

Serious people scare me. They have too much unhappiness in them. They complicate just to hide their loneliness. They get attached to routines as easily as to a domestic animal. They get used to forgetting to smile, because smiling makes them feel at the mercy of others. They risk nothing for nothing. They don't love. They don't dream. They hardly breathe. They are children of quiet people. Those who have no stories to tell. No love either. They only have a lot of complaints with a musty smell and tons of tears forgotten to cry. People who die without anyone noticing or caring. That's all. Nothing more.

I prefer a thousand times more to wake up hungover than sorry. The hangover is part of who I am whenever I lose myself at the bottom of a glass to forget a life that sometimes seems to pass too quickly. Regret exists in another sphere, in the world of the stupidity of believing that everything could have been different. If everything had been differently, maybe I wouldn't even be writing these lines. Maybe it would exist beyond this moment. In another time. In another place. Perhaps in a life of vices and plots, of debauchery and arrogance. We all have a natural tendency to shy away from that which is for us. It's part of our nature as imbeciles. We censor the details and we almost always end up with nothing. We curse the cross we claim to carry since birth as a fate we cannot change. I don't accept it. I can't stand such stupidity. I was born free and I will die free. When it's the end that's left for me, I want it to be a party without end. A laughter whose echo will last until after my death. For the rest of my life. And even more. For all my everlasting.

People leave our lives because we have to learn to live without them. It is the beginning of a new life, a life without those who miss us or have stubbornly left us behind. We have to teach ourselves to go down different paths. To go in search of what was always ours, of what until then we only wanted to look for with others. The truth is that we probably did not find anything significant, because to seek something with someone is to give them the power to decide many times what we are really going to find. Nothing has to be perfect, but just new. The time has come for us to choose everything differently. Our time has come to live more than just brief moments with us. The time has come for us to write a new story about who we can be. Without the others. Way beyond them.

Your health depends on who you believe you are. All your wrong thoughts about who you are generate terrible changes within you. Your whole body is sensitive to how you feel. Guilt, frustration, lies, resentment, fear, alter your inner balance, the way your organs and fluids listen to your soul. It is no use deceiving yourself with life. You gain little by hiding yourself where you think you cannot be seen. Time is not your ally here. What changes you is being in your joy. In your smile that is closest to your heart. The one that keeps you away from what is bad for you. The one that reminds you that there are no illnesses, only sick people.

You can be sure that what makes me who I am is not so much the courage to be myself, but rather the passion of wanting to be more and more myself, especially knowing how to live with my feet on the ground and my heart touching the sky at the same time, where I came from and where I will surely return to one day. Have no doubt that I no longer run away from anything, not because I no longer feel fear, but because I have understood that everything I do not face takes root in me and prevents me from accessing other places and times that have more to do with me. Let there be no doubt that I deserve the life I live, not because I am better than anyone else, but because I have not given up on what I felt was for me. I deserve me. I am part of a love and an endless poem. Of a story written for all my forever and ever.

To be happy you have to be stronger than a lot of unhappy shit. There's no way it can't be that way. There are always going to be people willing to say what was never said, to silence what was never even shouted, to lie to keep the truth out, to search for what was never meant to be gone. There will always be people with a strange urge to throw you down, to take revenge for what you can't make them feel, to make up excuses to make you look worse than you ever were. Your life is always desired by those who never told it to your face. Those who look you in the eye deserve you. The others are only who you allow them to be. Nothing else can surprise you or make you suffer.

Only those who have no dreams grow old. Those who go to bed without a smile. Who stop believing in new beginnings and stories. Those who stop wanting kisses in the middle of the night. Those who get used to complaining about everything they allow. Those who think too much about what they don't want. Those who no longer feel like falling asleep holding hands. Those who criticize more than they praise. Those who give up traveling. Those who refuse to listen to their heart. Those who insist on forcing a normality that is immediately perceived to be false. Those who let themselves die without ever having felt part of a life.

Don't be frightened by the sound of your wings flapping when you dare to start flying. Lift your head up and smile. Everything you will feel from here on out is new to you. Nothing is the same anymore. The world changes as soon as you lift your feet off the ground and gain height. Everything shrinks in size and takes on another shape. Nothing seems so big or strange to you any more. You see the outlines, the shadows and the angles and you are no longer frightened. The taller you feel, the braver you become. You no longer fear anything. You no longer want anything but to fly. To flap your wings and soar. The higher, the better. The faster, the greater the pleasure. Sharing space with the birds and the angels. Just with them. Far from hell. Closer to the heaven you were promised.

Don't let fear tie you to a place or to someone. You will suffer like few others. You'll put yourself at the mercy of what you've always avoided. There's no way it can't be that way. Your miserable state of acceptance reduces you to a dead-end thought. To a lost alley in your heart. Even your god can't make himself heard, because you have to call him first. You no longer have the strength to do so. You believe in so little that you always hit the same wall. The one you no longer know how to turn your back on. Standing next to your clock of hours and dreams that stopped working a long time ago.

Don't have any illusions. You will only remain in the memory of those who loved you. Everyone else will forget you because no one feels the absence of someone they don't miss at all. All memory is routine. Only what you engrave in your heart remains beyond remembrance. Only that becomes part of what you no longer forget. The rest is all that you neither choose nor remain in you. That which leaves without warning. Without taking you away. Without leaving any love.

I can't stand advice from people too wise. They are not crazy enough to feed my dreams. I like people who tell me without telling me, who show me without showing me, who make me without making me. I have no patience for people without passion. They bore me with their seriousness and the sum of lies with which they justify the lack of truth in their lives. I need someone on my side who can teach me to be even crazier. Someone who won't retouch words or adapt them to desires that never come true. I want with me someone who makes me laugh without measure. Who makes me live things that are so immense that I find it difficult to define. I like someone who enters my imagination and never leaves. Who condemns me to perpetual joy. And to much more. That I won't say.

It is of no use to me to invent paths or skies. My direction is made of strokes of life. The size of my luggage is always smaller than my journey. I already stop for a short time in each place. I am no longer one to put down roots. I let them stay in the land that saw me die for lack of life. I no longer belong to anyone. Not even to myself. I am a world outside the world. An adventure made of many adventures. A fugitive from sameness and submission. Someone who fights for nothing else. Who turns with what he has and creates. With whatever brings him inspiration. Without passport or borders. Without time or any dreams. Just with himself. Forever.

There are people who have the same shape as love. They awaken in us the rush to get to the beginning of everything. Even in silence, they speak to us. Their words make us hitchhike from memory to the places where hugs given without seconds or explanations prevail. Something in them extends us beyond where we are. They make us fly with closed eyes to what we feel touching our skin. They are not fingers, nor tongue. They are not lips, nor breath. They are moments. Times when love is everything without ceasing to be so much more. Things with meaning. Things that find us when we least expect them. Loves that tell us what is born again in us.

When I got married, I was only 23 years old. I was nervous, but at the same time apathetic. I had thrown up the day before a mixture of salty snack and freshly fermented sweet wine. I spent the night between thoughts of responsibility and escaping desires and an agony that could kill me. I really liked the one who was to become my wife, but there were already too many desires for freedom in me that were difficult to fulfil with someone on my side. Her unexpected pregnancy caught me totally unprepared and threw me into a pit of anxiety I had never felt before. The news of being a father frightened me, but also made me smile. When the morning of my wedding day showed through the holes in my bedroom shutter, the decision to stay had prevailed. So had the dizziness and agony.

It's fantastic to realise that with age I am becoming the person I always thought I would one day become. I have regained faith in what was previously indifferent to me. I have learned to listen to my innermost side, that side where my soul used to keep silent and now speaks without needing to be asked anything. I began not to doubt myself or what I choose to leave behind without hesitation. I have dared to follow my rebelliousness as a free man without being afraid of the opinion of others. I no longer give so much importance to details and ideas. I became a lover of attitudes and understood that I am all that remains after nothing else remains. Nobody teaches me any more. I just listen to the sky inside my chest.

We have a habit of choosing to live things almost always the hard way. No matter how much we say we want to do something differently, we seem to have a natural tendency towards difficulty. Complicating has become synonymous with knowing how to live. Simplifying is beginning to sound like an escape. Yet it is in simplification that lies the greatness of almost everything. Nothing becomes ours until we know its simpler side. There are loves that reveal themselves in a simple way, stories that are told in a simple way, people who behave in a simple way, places that are beautiful because they are so simple, dreams that become simple, and it is in listing them that we immediately understand that what links them together is the simplicity of everything that is timeless. And the timelessness of what is simple is manifested in everything that lives without past or future, without itineraries or pretensions, without sadness or resentment. It manifests itself in the greater or lesser will of each one to find the time to simplify that which until today has seemed difficult.

There are orgasms that are not of this world. They would be said to have a life of their own in such a way that they tear the flesh from my bones, boil the air in my lungs, unravel my ideas and time, make me feel part of what I no longer know in myself. My heart seems to stop so fast. My eyes open to see what they no longer know they are seeing. My arms grab you without measuring the strength or duration of my grip any longer. I run without moving, I fly without gaining height, I speak without understanding myself, I cry out to a god for an intervention I don't desire, I die of a pleasure that never kills me. There are orgasms that are not of this world.

Don't show me how you want me to be, because I won't pay any attention to you. Don't tell me what you want me to do, because I'll always do as I please. Don't want to fool me, because you'll only get close once. Don't waste time judging me, because I stopped believing in you a long time ago. I know it may seem insolent, but I see everything differently now. Many people no longer need me and I no longer run away from the moments when I only need me. I chose to stay close to the ground that shelters me when I fall. I keep the smell of it in my heart every time I get up. It has become part of me. Like everything that sets me free. Between many truths and some secrets.

For a long time I found it difficult to accept myself because I didn't feel loved as a child. I don't blame anyone. I don't need it, and I don't want it. I cannot be loved by those who do not love themselves. I was cared for and learned to create a world where I felt safer. I grew up looking like who I didn't feel inside. I believed no one could understand that I was insecure and very much alone. One day, I made peace with everything that made me suffer and left on my own. I turned my back on what no longer made me cry or smile and went to write my story. I soiled many sheets of paper. I broke many pens. I tore chapters and erased too many lines. I did a lot without really knowing what I was doing. I did everything in search of what life put in my way. I met demons and angels. Light and shadows. Passions and illusions. Memories and forgetfulness. A life that I made to suit myself and no one else. Like the bottom of my pockets. Full of everything and without fear of losing anything.

Accept trying without the outcome being important. Try and stay. Don't try anything to get somewhere. Just try because it makes sense for you to try. That is all. Try and wait for what life will show you next. Only then will you understand whether you should continue in this direction or change your choice. That is what trying is. It means taking the risk of opening your arms without wanting to know what you will embrace. It means having the time not to be in a hurry to get wherever you are.

My heart is wild, not because it beats uncompromisingly, but because it is untamable and only smiles at those who want it to or those who captivate it with their simplicity and rebelliousness. Each beat is unrepeatable. Each step is taken only in freedom. Each feeling is always great, intense, because that was the way I chose to live my whole story down here. When I leave, I take memories with the taste of life. Only life. Only life and nothing else.

Only those who have never loved envy. What I say is not unreasonable. After all, I have already heard so much stupidity that I don't have to listen to anymore. They accuse me of being indifferent to those who suffer and to those who pay no attention to me. They insist on wanting to live my life even more than I do. It's funny how they worry about depriving me of what I probably don't even have. They create images and scenarios about who I am and what I do as if they were seers and oracle makers, wizards even. They pass by me with the solemnity of priests or musicians in unemployment and can't help but look at me out of the corner of their eye. They make me smile. I can't take them very seriously. Forgive me if it's the opposite you're looking for. In that case, smile at me, not as if you were doing it to a god, because I never was, but because you have stopped feeling embarrassed by someone who wants nothing from anyone, let alone what they don't have to give me. I want only what is simple and light. What defines every particle of who I am being. I want to always be available for life. To mine. Of course. Because I only live what I embrace. No less. No more.

I'm not selling anything. In fact, I don't sell or want to sell anything. I only talk about what I believe in. I have no time for set phrases or to please those who persist in the illusion of a truth glued to saliva. Those who know me know what I am talking about. Those who do not know me, let them come and meet me. I am always here for those who wish to go further in their daring to live and in their will to face fears and senseless illusions. Life is too precious to waste. Time is too vague to be taken into account. The important thing is this moment, because it is now that you can define what you will choose to do next. The rest are detours. Boundaries and moats. Choices you make to stop yourself from choosing.

Sometimes I forget how old I am. The truth is that I stopped growing old the day I felt the warmth of my smile on my face again. I don't remember exactly when that moment was. I believe it was several, added to and subtracted by my willingness to step outside the predictable and the obvious. I know I felt each one of them as a victory over the stupidity of wanting to remain indifferent to the life that was pulsating inside and outside of me. It was then that I let my hair grow out, threw away all the clothes that reminded me or kept me clinging to a past of fear and lack of courage, went back to wearing jeans half unbuttoned and unironed and old trainers so I could run or jump again if I felt like it. What set me apart was the ability to do what I hadn't done for a long time due to shame or lack of confidence. I began to stop fooling myself with lies and half-truths and to celebrate every minute of my life without fear that it was my last. Nothing else has stayed the same. Not even the measure of time and years. Everything gained the brief instant that only eternity can match. The instant in which I managed to fill with smiles what before was only silence and pain.

Flying is much more than flapping wings and taking off. Flying is to free myself from meaningless stories and dreams without truth. It is to go where I want to go without anyone stopping me or demanding anything. It is having the ability to create new perspectives and words to live the unthinkable and the unpredictable. When I let myself fly, I climb up to where few others reach, only because I began to believe in my side as an angel without wings, in my talent for flying above the clouds, right next to my sky. Flying is above all not being afraid of falling. It is to risk more and more following your heart. Here and now. Always. Without fear of any pain. Without fear of anything.

Don't take anything that you are not prepared for the eventuality that you might lose it. Do not force yourself to believe in anything that does not make sense to you. Never give up your sensitivity, even if it exposes you to what you never thought you would experience. Remember that all the fear you feel serves above all to free the love that you still do not know you feel for yourself. Do not run away from loneliness, because it is through it that you find your way. I know that this may seem a contradiction in terms, but the truth is that only in the presence of solitude can you be entirely with yourself. With nothing else. Not even with love. Not even before death. Not even with that which you do not yet know, but which you stubbornly want.

I like it when I feel empty, because the feeling always precedes some change. Change seduces me. It's part of my more irreverent and inconsequential side. It excites me. It rips my chest open with desires and longings for new skies and flights never before made. Emptiness does not mean that I have nothing. It means that I have some space inside me that will soon be filled.

The consciousness I have of myself happens because I am something or someone outside of who I believe I am. You are only aware of that which is not part of you. I am aware of my body because it is not really mine. I am aware of my thoughts because I am not really the one who thinks them. The truth is that I am only a consciousness in a process of interaction with the world outside myself. I am a consciousness with nothing, because nothing is part of me. Everything exists outside of me. I am just the consciousness, the energy, the light, that interacts with everything not to connect with anything, but only to feel. To live the emotions that everything around me makes me feel in the realisation that everything exists only to enable me to find the natural state of peace and happiness that exists within me, only within me, without worries of any kind. I am a consciousness and nothing more. A soul, if you will. An energy that seeks its own energy in communion with all other things around it. That is the challenge. That is the provocation. To be who I am without wanting to be anything else.

When I changed my life, many people disappeared without a word. Or worse. Without being able to avoid from the get-go cruel words of contempt, disinterest and bad luck. They vowed me a death foretold. A poor man's fate. When I began to write my new story and stopped remembering them, when I forgave myself for the disappointment I felt, they returned as if nothing had happened. I couldn't dodge closing the door and all the windows on them, because hypocrisy is the worst of all vomit. Of all the shit. For me.

I can never resist your smile. I lose myself in the way the movement of your lips accompanies that of your eyes. I long for your kiss, your mouth's touch. The life you beckon me with. I want to feel between my fingers the hair that contours your gaze where fire and the sensuality of an invitation that I never tire of pouring over my body come together. There is a sky that opens up every time we open our arms. Whenever your breasts mark my chest. You draw a smile. Just one. Always the same. The one who knows I can't resist you. My woman. My whore. My restlessness. My calm.

I am the one who writes my life. Of that I no longer have any doubts. I don't believe in karma and destiny, nor in compulsory paths. I believe in new opportunities and choices. I no longer have any doubts about my talent for choosing what I want, even if I am told that there are choices I am forced to make. Nothing and no one forces me to do anything. I am free to choose to live in fear or self respect. The rest is all bullshit to delude me, to make me feel bad and seek acceptance from others. I don't fall for that anymore. To belo with what others want for me. I've learned to choose what my heart asks me and my soul inspires me. To smile with emotion. Always. Because nothing else is so worthwhile.

It is essential not to forget that the important thing is not theories, but exceptions, because it is through them that everything gains a new perspective and new and great journeys begin. The problem with theories is that they cast the world into a predictable and monotonous sameness. I have always had great difficulty in flipping through manuals and instruction books. I'd rather wreck a machine trying to explore all its possibilities than follow safety and maintenance rules. I know I may sound like a madman, but the truth is I don't do well with the precariousness of what little we like to know and use. I need to always follow the call of life. I want to know more and more about my world. I can't contradict this desire of mine. Nor deny it. It is stronger than everything. It is me in my purest form of living. Without fear. Without the will to run away. Writing great stories in my adventurous heart to one day leave without the fear of never coming back.

I've long since stopped asking myself questions. It's a total waste of time. Answers always come when I expect nothing. I don't stand by either. I only do what has to do with me. To do otherwise is to want to live several lives in one. It's turning my life into one big effort and one giant battle where wanting to win is my biggest defeat. I have also stopped long ago from wanting to interpret the signs. I am attentive only to what I feel, because to feel is to understand the simplicity of each thing. It's seeing myself in each thing. It's not wanting anything, because I already have everything.

There is always more than one way to express the same emotion, but only one way to deny it. You deny an emotion when you are afraid of it. When you do not let it access your soul. When you place expectations where you should only place new possibilities. All emotions are to be lived. They are meant to keep you from becoming stagnant in the things you know and have always done. They are there to enable you to move forward instead of backwards and to live with less and less fear. They are so that you can recognise yourself in each and every one of your heart's answers. All of this and much more. That which is for you. Since always.

I don't say this out of presumption, but there are people who are afraid of what I write, speak and who I have become. They fear me because I disturb their lie. They criticise me because I smile at their seriousness. They judge me because it's the easiest way to deny what they don't want to feel. I don't ask them to like me either. I know very well the world I live in. I've always preferred simple people to idiots. I've always liked those who ignore me more than those who try to upset me. They can't do it, but they show what moves them. What makes them cry without tears. What makes them want to be like me.

One day, I'm going to leave. I've known that for a long time. I feel it deep inside me. My life won't always be around here. There's a place somewhere that waits for me. I don't know where it is, but I'm not worried about knowing it yet either. I know that it is where I will live the days that separate me from my death. They will be many, because I feel that I came here to be a bit of almost everything that sets me free. I know that I will live what is destined for me as a consequence of all the choices I have been making in my life. I realise that I am already closer. Much closer. I feel it with greater clarity in my chest with each passing day. The truth is that I'm in no hurry to get there either. I just don't want to waste any more time.

One part of me is certainty and the other part is adventure. I anticipate the world without being part of it. My uncertainty and my sameness ended the day I became aware of the existence of my soul. I stopped being a normal guy as soon as I heard its voice for the first time. I understood the full magnificence of who I am in its provocations and requests. I realised that if I don't follow my truth I am just an intrusion of what I want to be. Without my truth, I become an eternal hostage of fear. A wanderer without a heart. A spirit trapped in a future that will never be present.

My biggest mistake was to think that I could not make a mistake when it is essential to make a mistake. There is always a good dose of eroticism and sensuality in every mistake, precisely because it lays me bare before myself. It exposes me as nothing and no one else can. It allows me to correct my stupid will of not wanting to fail. It judges me mercilessly and with the brutality of a slap in the face. It makes me feel like I'm repeating what I've said before I wouldn't do anymore. It works like a drug in time of hangover. It brings me back to reality. It gives me what only a mistake is allowed to give me. It gives me the chance to try one more time.

I don't believe much in words and feelings anymore, but in what people are willing to do to show them. I like those who give me the feeling that time has stopped without having to say anything to me. I like those who show me what they feel without having to say anything. Sometimes it is enough that they hold me in one of those embraces that last as long as a smile. A kiss. Just a kiss.

Book a trip and set off without looking back. Discover who you are in a place you never thought you'd go. There is magic in the unknown and the unexpected. The sense of yourself becomes easier to understand as a traveller. Nothing is familiar or habitual. You can finally feel as you have never felt all the things you have never seen. Your freedom takes on a new colour. You are free to take all directions and to stop whenever you feel like it. Nothing and nobody can stop you. When you travel, you understand much of what you had given up understanding about yourself. Even your shadow becomes different under an unknown sun. It takes on an outline of new life.

There are miracles that are proclaimed even before they happen. There are secrets that are revealed even before they are created. There are loves that are born before they are conceived. There are places we choose before we even know they exist. There are people who know each other even before they have seen each other. **Everything that exists today has existed before. It is the geography of life, where everything is an inexplicable longing to live what has already been lived before. Perhaps things that happened in another life. Perhaps in another time. Surely, beyond all that is known. Beyond everything you do.**

The worst thing they can do to me is to want to shut my soul up. I always find it very difficult to explain what I feel. It's almost the domain of the unspeakable, the inexplicable. It's the lack of everything that defines me. The truth is that I don't know how to live without being in accordance with my soul. Everything it makes me feel inside my heart is what distinguishes me from the rest of the world. It is my emotional identity card. My passport to life. My ticket to heaven. A voice with a life of its own. Just like mine. Simply.

The best answers are given with the eyes. No words or gestures are necessary. Not even questions. The eyes are the perfect equation capable of everything. The place of all emotions and secrets. The silence that can stop time or make it disappear without a trace. The scream of those who do not want to speak or say what they feel. The unforgettable moment when some look at me. When some call me. Yours. Only yours. Only yours. The only ones that make me return from where I never wanted to stay. From far away from you. From places where the memory of your look smells of longing. Of pain. From everything else that has nothing to do with you. Far away from me. Always too far from me.

There is no point in me knowing my loneliness if I don't accept it as part of my life. The fear of being alone has never scared me. I have always understood that there will be times when my desire to be alone will far outweigh my desire for companionship. I have always been a loner. I love my company. I don't mind at all staying in my corner writing, listening to music, drinking a glass of red wine and talking quietly to myself. I think better alone. Thoughts are in no hurry to get anywhere. They are an extension of my calm. A simple definition of how I see and feel. An intimate relationship with my own intimacy. A sign that I love being with myself. That's all.

I am made of a smile that only I know how to smile. I learned to smile when I started to feel what's in my soul. Writing came soon after. Writing made me even more true to myself. It taught me that lying is the stupidest way to fear the truth. I no longer fear the opinion of others. I no longer seek their approval. I am beautiful in my own way. I don't follow fashions or orders. I don't wear disguises. I love what I love and respect what I don't love. I am sensitive to people's rebelliousness and to a skin with skin vices. I don't believe in life without provocation. I love my freedom. I respect everyone's choices. I always protect myself from some people. I don't fear envy or cursing, but I don't let them get on my side. I don't do anything for the middle ground. Parts annoy me. I always prefer the whole. The whole of me. Without discarding anything. Even nothing.

A difficult love is not a love. It is a weariness. It is an illusion believed out of stupidity. It's a fight without a winner. Whoever chooses to live a difficult love is a perfect imbecile. The fantasy of wanting to turn a frog into a prince or a princess is even more idiotic than that of giving pearls to pigs. It's a guaranteed certificate of suffering. It's a desire to want to change something that was never anything. Living a difficult love is not wanting to live any love. It's living without having the courage to question what you feel. It's wishing for what you will never understand.

The fantastic is always non-transferable. No one can feel what I feel. Not even in love. Not even in pain. The fantastic is like a very personal secret. It belongs only to me. Only I know what I feel and no one else. It's not possible to be differently. I can't tell someone how it is, because I'll never know how to explain it. The fantastic can never be explained. You risk touching it. You run after it. You don't let it die. It engraves itself like a tattoo. Not on the skin. Rather in the most intimate part of each person. There, where nothing is impossible. There, where the most futile becomes important.

If it's a sleepless night, let it be dreaming about you. I hate spending every waking hour staring at the ceiling and doing nothing but thinking of stupid, unresolved things. I prefer you to fill my sleepless time. I love closing my eyes and letting you lie on my side of the bed. I love the way you rest your head on my chest and touch my sex on the inside of my pajama trousers. There's something sinful about the play of your fingers that I give in to without saying anything. I can't help stretching my neck a little when your hand vehemently grips the entire space between my thighs. All my fantasies are dependent on your next moves. I await them with the caution of one who expects what she does not know, when the truth is that I know them all too well. What pleases me is my momentary lack of memory. It makes me crave even more every touch you'll give me and every thrust you tend to draw slowly on my hard-on. I'm like that. I can't say no to you. I never want to say no to you.

I believe that temptations are made to give in to them. All prohibitions take the air out of me. They squeeze my heart too tightly and I always find it hard to stay alive. There are secret desires in all temptations. There are more than enough reasons to give in to them. The more so because they are never habits. They are always and only provocations.

The best thing about trying is not caring about succeeding. The best thing about trying is the joy of simply trying. When I try, I feel alive. Not trying is like repeating an echo without leaving the place. Nothing changes. Nothing inspires to anything. Trying is not accepting to be still. It is a homage to life. It is to let the tears that precede every smile fall freely. It is not seeking answers or even asking questions. It is simply to go. Without fear of not coming back.

Normal people scare me. They always bear a striking resemblance to an instruction manual. They don't seem to know how to move without the predictability of all those who live in fear of life. They fear almost every new opportunity because it can take away some of the little they believe they have. They need to be like almost everyone else, to do what everyone else does, to talk about what everyone else talks about. Difference works on them like a disease. A curse that they need to exorcise by any means and as soon as possible. I always find it very difficult to be at the same party, in the same room, at the same table with normal people. I am strangely tempted each time to manifest my provocative side. My penchant for messing with everything that is pre-established or assumed is abhorrent. I can't sit still or shut up. I have always been too sensitive to the waste of life.

I am under no obligation to make sense to anyone. Every man and woman is different from me in many ways. We don't necessarily have to have common ground or empathies. Our paths may well tend to be in opposite or divergent directions. Nor do we need to condemn ourselves to oblivion to each other, or force ourselves to isolate ourselves from everyone else. In fact, I believe I only make sense to those who find answers in what I say and write. Not in who I am or who I represent. If that were the case, we would have a hard time distinguishing between us by similarities. The problem is that too many people represent the same or something very similar. They lack the spontaneity. The lack of fear. The courage to not want to make sense to anyone.

The intensity of each madness is in the dimension of the passion with which I commit it. For a long time now I have not been satisfied with things that are more or less or that do not leave a mark on me. I always prefer those that make my skin crawl without touching them. The apparently useless ones which later prove to be indispensable. Those that make me smile before even being close to me. The ones that only give me certainty at the end. The ones I haven't done yet, but which belong to me since I started thinking about them. I like above all the crazy things that not even I know are crazy. The ones that surprise me by the way they possess me. The ones that inspire me. The ones that make me crazy with joy for not knowing how to live without them. As if they were my greatest loves. Or more than that. Inseparable parts of myself. Of my heart.

I am made of each of the intense parts of all my loves. Each woman left in me what no other could. My skin and soul are etched from one end to the other with the words they said to me and I never forgot. I probably didn't love them as they deserved, but I was always generous in the measure of what they made me feel. Love is also possible that way. At least for me. I believe it was also for all those who lived it with me. What I have learned from each of them is that I can love without realising that I am really loving. They say it's my kisses that give away my love. I believe it. Everything that is love in me is always written with a story of kisses. I have no other way. I don't know how to do it any other way.

No one knows true love until they accept the chance to live without it. The desire to want to love someone often leads to a very different reality. All that one seeks is not always what one needs. Sometimes you want things that will never be yours, not even if you want them badly enough. The truth is that everything we do for love defines us in its absence. You cannot love someone without loving yourself equally. We always want to love in the measure of the impossible. So we love in others what we would like to be ours. There's no way it can't be that way. Just like almost everything else in life. Too often we want that which we will never be able to love. Or even feel.

Have fun until every moment of your life is a lifetime. Live each passion as if it was always the first. Learn to leave without looking back. Look at the sky whenever you can, because it is from there that the stars fall without hurting you. Fly without taking your feet off the ground so that nothing that you love is far from you. Write a diary. Don't want to find the reason for many of your smiles. Drink only with those who make you celebrate life. Leave nothing undone of what your soul asks of you and everything will be all right. No one will take away from you what you have lived. Only what you have not yet done. Eventually.

I like a point of view without limits. It always reminds me of the life I still want to live. The things I don't want to take for granted. The passion for everything that makes me go. The need to keep writing about what I feel. The crazy things I haven't tried yet. The paths beyond the ones I have already walked. The places where I want to lose myself with you. The perversions and desires of my soul. The sentences I won't carry out. The nights that I will love smiling. Everything that is definitive and I refuse to accept without a fight. Everything that is still nothing to me, but also without yet ceasing to be everything. Like tears kept out of my eyes. Like angels with invisible wings. Like you and me. Just you and me.

You only find those who are also looking for you. But don't search in order to be found. Seek rather so that you may find yourself. What comes after is a consequence of what you never questioned. Or felt. Thanks be to God. Or to you. Whatever. The important thing is you above anyone else. Only you. Just you. With all the sum of yourself. Of what you learn. Of how you love yourself. Of what you will never forget wanting to give to others.

My conscience is clear. I am not perfect, but neither have I promised anyone to be. My world is reduced to what I feel and desire. Also what I do, which is the result of who I really am. The rest is only part of the imagination of those who love or hate me. To the sense of humour of those who think they know me. It matters little to me. I am not perfect, nor have I ever claimed to be. My life is perfect, otherwise it would be otherwise. No doubt about it.

Smiling only depends on me. It's no longer something I hand over to anyone. It is an intimate part of who I have become. Like my body. My heart. Because smiling is exposing myself in what I feel. What I like to share. It is to make it part of who also receives it. Conversely, to smile alone is to be grateful for what you understand. I've smiled for things I accepted before I even understood them. For desires and loves that I did not know how to live. For the lack of a smile from some people. I have smiled alone many times. Not because I feel lonely. Just because my smile no longer belongs to those who want to take it away from me. Nor from those who cry at my happiness.

I am as free as I like to be. Every moment of my life is precious and unequalled. Nothing repeats. Everything is a time of new experiences, choices and smiles. There is little that frightens me anymore. I live each minute, each instant, with the intensity of someone who is not afraid of losing anything. Because nothing is mine. Everything is lent to me by life to enjoy until the end. Like on a game board where I never lose. Where I only win. Because that's what happiness is. A certainty that everything can change from one moment to the next, but that nothing can change who I truly am.

I believe that there is no right time to start loving. It is not programmed like a task or a machine. You realise that it has arrived, in that space of time without any reason or logic. You feel it because it has become a desire without having wanted it before. A vertigo without abyss. A promise immediately fulfilled. An absence of doubt that the time to start loving is any hour. It is not a bizarre thing, nor a moment of the heart alone. It is something that transcends us, but is also deep inside us. Like a clock with a life of its own. A muscle turned inside out. A vein filled with blood like no other. A soul free at last to be truly a soul. In an hour that in the end could not have been any other. The hour when love was found. No other hour so hourly.

The moment of change for many happens when their heart breaks into a thousand and one pieces of pain. The feeling is that you no longer have any present or future. Everything ends there. Like a death that keeps us alive only to continue suffering. As if heaven forgot us or wanted to avoid us. Just like that. When I see people at this point, I understand that their moment of change is coming. I only ask that they too understand. Not to give up. Not to become extras in new plots. Of new escapes.

There was a time when I wanted to help others before helping myself. It's not something you can forget. When you do something for the first time, nothing that happens next is what you truly imagined. The same thing happens when you believe in others before you get to know them. The possibility of things being as you want them to be is a perfect state of illusion. Nothing happens as one thinks it will. Nothing is the same as anything else. It seems that life has come together to fuck us by the hand of who we want on our side the most. The truth is, I no longer want on my side anyone who makes me feel even more alone or unloved. I prefer to continue on my path with me. To be even freer. To be even crazier. Absurdly like myself.

I like a woman who knows how to hold me. Who touches my soul without squeezing my body too tightly. Who makes me feel her arms around my torso and her hands firmly on my back. I like a woman who undresses me with her embrace without taking my clothes off. Who excites me and makes me be where I am not yet. That tears my lips without kissing me. Who desires me without telling me. Of a woman whose embrace makes me restless and steals my silence. I like a woman. A woman who knows how to embrace me. A woman who comes to life in my embrace.

Everything that I don't have today is entirely my responsibility. What I do defines what comes to me. If I don't do it for myself but only for others, I won't receive what has to do with me. If I do it for me without wanting to harm anyone, I will only receive what has to do with who I am. All my wishes come true if I don't worry about what others expect from me. If I only want to be happy. If I want to get closer and closer to my essence and my mission. In a commitment with me. Only with me. With nobody else.

I like to lose my sobriety without getting drunk, to stay at that point where I smile at what I didn't smile at before, where I talk about everything as the connoisseur that I am not. The truth is that it is at that point that I feel closer to what I rarely see so closely. Everything seems to become more accessible instead of more distant. Drunkenness without losing sobriety helps me to access my more shameless, more debauched side, the one I only show to whom I want, when I feel like it. I say when I feel like it, because there are times when sobriety takes away my courage completely. Not because I'm ever afraid of going there. Only because to get there I have to be drunk without ceasing to be sober to feel in others what moves me most inside. Their debauchery. Their desire to also want to feel my darker side.

All our problems start when we allow what is not supposed to be allowed. Life gets more and more bashful and difficult. Excuses and accusations take over who we have become. We come to believe in what reduces us and we no longer dream of what used to make us smile. We come up against the comfort of knowing that there are many more like ourselves or even worse. It is a sad consolation for those who forget more easily than remember who once wanted to be so much. I don't know why problems make us give up so quickly. It seems we choose them for that purpose. Or else to feel that we will never be alone in the failure of living as owners of a destiny with a too short shelf life.

What distinguishes me from others does not make me better than anyone else. It just makes me different. Different from all those who do not know how to be different. Different from all those who do not understand that everything about me is nothing more than the way in which life has chosen to manifest itself through me. I am not and do not aspire to be more this or more that. I love life too much to limit it to goals. I want what it alone can give me. I want to live it. I just want to live it. As if death didn't exist. Not because I'm afraid of dying. I know that one day I'll be gone. My body will recognize the ballet of its end. My soul will fly to where one day it promised to return. But as long as I feel alive, I don't want to be put where I am not yet. Nor to be made who I am not. Really. I want to be left alone. To not demand anything from me. I want them to fuck off.

To see illness as a misfortune is to understand nothing at all about life. To understand that illness is a salvation is not for many. To realise that through illness one can begin a cure for what was already ill even before the illness is a privilege accessible only to those who do not fear death. Not being afraid of falling ill is only for those who know how to live differently from what is expected of everyone. It is only for those for whom an illness is an inevitable path to another path. The one that was distant. The one that is missed. That of life. That of consciousness. That of awakening. So this. So only this.

Survival can never be a purpose, because without purpose nothing happens that is worth remembering. Without a purpose, you don't have a mission. In fact, one has very little of almost nothing. There must be a time for everything but survival. Survival is the lack of time to live. Or of will. Or of wanting. Because living is not for everyone. It is for those who choose to move forward when everyone else chooses to close their eyes.

Around you, time stops. It ceases to exist. It is a sum of kisses and smells of love. Of smiles and silences upon waking up. It is an ambiguous prophecy that only exists when we are not together, in the stubbornness of wanting to transform every second of our absence into a desire for more time. An uncontrolled longing for everything that we only live when we are in each other's arms. In the bed that shelters us. In the morning that baptises us in light. Often without speaking. Just holding hands. In a desire that time always stays behind us. Not as a shadow. Rather as something that allows us to live away from any time other than our own.

I live for fun. For a long time now. I don't know how to live any other way. I have fun from the soul. From what makes it smile. That's it and nothing else. I no longer allow myself detours or sudden braking. I always live what I feel and rarely what I think. It is a truculent exercise. Difficult. But I have learnt how to make it possible. I have transformed it into a delicate and intense part of me. Like everything else in my life. In that all-consuming desire to be happy. No more or less than anyone else. Happy in the measure of everything I feel. Of nothing of what I think.

Democracy is the best of regimes at professing false freedom, at being able to hide any half-truth with many lies and at abusing power as an excuse to change the lives of its citizens. It is perhaps also the only one that lets me write these words. If I lived or was born in a country where civil rights were forgotten and torture was the most common side of life for the few who dared to speak more than five sentences in a row on any given topic, I probably wouldn't have lived more than my first twenty years. I would almost certainly have been killed in the first confrontation of ideas in public. I don't know how to keep quiet in the face of injustice or abuse. I have always known that being different from the majority I am forced to pay a much higher price than the mediocre and the cowardly. I don't mind either. If I'm going to die, let it be from so much living.

The certainty that many more people recognise me in the street is a very strange but also pleasant feeling. Strange, because it is something I never thought I would experience. Pleasant, because I see in the eyes of those who look at me the most distinct emotions. Some people are immediately happy to meet me, but they don't come closer. Others cannot hide a trace of forced indifference or discomfort when they see me. Still others get nervous and mutter unnoticed words about my presence. Still others, the kindest ones, come up to me and exchange half a dozen words of contentment and spontaneity. Being known is by no means a curse. It is a way of testing my humility. A way of reminding myself who I am. Who I don't want to stop being.

I can't stand queues. Nor conversations to pass the time. Nor days without light. I can't stand nostalgic memories of those who complain about everything. Nor screams from spoilt and ill-mannered children. Nor those who think too much about unimportant things. I have no time for what I don't love. Nor for those who want to deify me. Or to judge. Where the simplest is distorted and the most obvious is questioned. I don't feel like being with those who run away from improvisation or the unexpected. Where everything is weighed and thought through before it happens. Like a habit. Or a plan. Anything else planned and more than planned. What the hell. I'd rather go crazy than be like everyone else. I don't want to be like those who think they are more than me. I prefer a thousand times the silence of the deaf to the stupidity of those who don't know what they're saying.

Maturity does not develop with age, but in the attitude one chooses to have towards oneself. People only understand what is within the range of their perception. Everything that one wants to know about oneself depends on what one believes about oneself. To be mature is to have a sense of responsibility to be unique. Nobody is supposed to do the same as the other. Immaturity exists in the need for comparison on different levels. Wanting to do as the other does. Wanting to be who the other is. None of that can work. To be a copy is the worst sin. It is a death that in nothing resembles a life in those who seek awards where there are no races. Not even championships. Where there is only repetition. Habits of staying so as not to think of leaving.

I melt with those who see me make mistakes and tell me that I am brave for trying. I smile whenever someone tells me about love, because talking about love always makes me find my best smile. I am touched by those who know that the greatest wounds are those that open my eyes and not those that lacerate my flesh. I am attracted to those who don't ask me for anything because they know that I am already giving them everything they will never ask me for. I love those who don't ask me to love them because they understand that only I can create my own way of feeling love. I stay only with those who ask me to stay, but who also never stop me from leaving. In one way or another, I am all this and much more that I don't want to make known yet. I believe that only mysteries perpetuate me in life.

I can't stand the smell of damp and old things. It feels like life has died out there and left a trail of mould and shadows. I can't touch anything. I go in and out with the quickness of someone who fears contracting some disease by breathing that mixture of dust and lack of use. I need light and colour. Everything that is new and smells clean. Maybe that's why I run away from visits to old museums and churches closed between damp and cold walls. Everything about them terrifies me. It makes me plan a thousand and one escapes before I even get in. There is nothing worse than that which seems to die in the same place it was born. It always kills a part of who I don't want to be. Or see.

My longing is mine alone. I don't share it with anyone. I believe that only I feel it inside me and that only I should disentangle myself in the midst of it. It is like a living being that lodges itself in the centre of my chest and prevents me from accepting the normal rules of the game. I don't believe that longing is love. Or lack. It's some fucking thing that makes me vulnerable in time and distance. I prefer to feel pain. I've already learned how to heal it. I know how it ends.

Everything that is intense strips me of resistance. I've always felt connected to everything that breathes intensity. It makes the skin on the back of my neck tingle and move forward. Only those who don't like intensity are incapable of dreaming. Dreams are only dreams if there is within them the will to make up for the lack of intensity in life. All intensity is a bond. A rescue. A detachment from love and an emancipation of the skin. A feeling that activates inspiration and daring. A desire for more, but each time even more. Even more like me. Intense like me.

I remembered the other day that there was a moment in my teenage years when I wanted to be a writer. I had just read

Hemingway's The Green Hills of Africa and travelled through much of who I was without yet being one. An adventurer of the unknown, an explorer of the art of daring to go where few others went, of facing the greatest dangers without fear of being hurt or even dying. I remember that afterwards I wrote some poems and dedicated them to each of my brief loves. I experienced the pleasant feeling of being older and wiser. Someone who remembers a past where there was a time for everything and for each thing. When I read one of my poems to a friend and received a silence of ignorance and disapproval from her, I put down the pen for another twenty years. It wasn't the time yet. Everything was still very black and white.

I no longer worry about the opportunities I missed. I always believe that I didn't choose them for some reason. All this can be seen as third-rate semantics, but I've never been one to waste time with ifs and maybes. I can't change anything I've done or stopped doing. What I can do is accept it. That's it and nothing more. It is in acceptance that all change begins. That is when everything finally begins to make sense. Like two parts of a map finally coming together. Without the need for any further annotation. Without needing anything else.

I like those who dream as if they were going to live forever. I take my hat off to those who leave when everyone tells them not to. I confess to admiring those who love the one they don't know. I see myself in those who pursue their path without fear of rain or thunderstorms. I am a fan of those who believe in themselves and always listen to what they feel. Once upon a time I did what I could. Today, I only don't do what is not about me. Most people say little to me anymore, not because I've become better than anyone else, but because I'm no longer afraid to be a loner among crowds. The truth is I don't need anyone. It's enough for me who stays with me.

To love without memory or revenge is what brings us closer to life. Accepting that the unknown is our place by birth makes us think less about the consequences of our choices. To be free is to understand that to love is above all to live without fear of living. Living without restrictions. Living to live. As one breathes. How you feel. Forever. Only.

Today I was told in no uncertain terms how old I was going to die. I was somewhat indignant, because I didn't ask, but I still managed to smile. I don't know, nor do I question, the talent of the person who can feel the time of my death. I have no problem with that. It is not the end of my life that interests me, but everything that I will be and do during that time. I believe in my capacity to live each day as if it were the best of all. I also know that death is a moment that no one will escape. When mine comes, may I be able to look back and smile. Nothing will give me greater pleasure. Of course. Above all for not having allowed myself to die before my death.

When my father and brother passed away, I didn't wear black to the funeral. I never thought it was appropriate. I love those who add lightness to the moment by wearing white. I didn't, only because I have almost no white clothes and I'm not in favour of anyone buying clothes for a funeral. I took a blue t-shirt, jeans and trainers, bracelets on my arm and my hair was loose. I didn't go that way to shock anyone or provoke anyone. I went that way because the pain was only in my heart. And even he wasn't wearing black. He was sad, but full of colour. He had a huge light inside him. A light that only comes out when you know that someone who is suffering is finally coming home.

I can't help having a perverse side. It's a side of me that wants to know the other side of everything. A side that dares to take me even further than I ever was. A side that wants to know more about so much more of myself. The one I rarely am in front of others. Of the one I am only with those who legitimise themselves in my perversion. In a parallel world where only those I allow enter. Who I want. Like a secret club. A secret. Like the most genuine of my truths.

Making time for your children without ceasing to feel love for you is the best way to grow old with a smile. I have two of my children living with me. The older ones. I believe they will soon go their own way. Nothing will ever be the same again, yet everything can continue to be different. There is a life that begins when I am alone with myself. It doesn't scare me at all to live alone. Part of my freedom is made that way. The other, is everything else.

Those who do not believe in the truth are usually afraid of it. Fear makes one lose all chances of making something different. In fact, it is easier to lie in order not to show how you feel about what you fear than to say what you are feeling. I have heard truths that sounded like lies to me without being able to say anything. There is a very own seduction that immediately shuts me up in the lies told to deny a truth. They manage to sound like a truce without being one. They find a way to be even more convincing than any truth. Even in the truth of being only lies.

We had a dobermann for sixteen years. She was one of the most docile animals I have ever met. Her size always made you think otherwise. No one would go near her, least of all if she remembered to bark. She had a loud and intimidating bark, so different from the happy wagging of her stumpy tail when she saw us coming home. She would jump on us and almost throw us to the ground. You had to be extraordinarily strong to withstand its impact without falling over. Sadly, with age she became deaf. She began to walk with her nose in the air, as if she had started to listen with her nose. When she left, she left a void in all of us. For a long time, we thought we heard her nails on the wooden floor upstairs. Maybe it was her spirit back home. Or our wish that she was never gone. Love for animals is like that. It has no end. It doesn't leave with them. Unfortunately.

The worst is what remains silent inside a heart. That which cannot be said. What pain has made you stop believing. What one gives up on seeing differently. A silent heart is made of absences and things not understood. Of memories and forgetfulness. It is made in the consciousness that time passes and never gives up its path. That there is no going back. That everything that has happened no longer finds the same road to return to. A heart that does not speak is a heart that is half alive. Dead because it can no longer say anything.

Relationships end because they never really were relationships. What was called love was never really love. It was anything but love. It was passion, possession, horniness or interest, but it was never love. If it was love, it would never have been a relationship either. It would always be something nameless, because where there is love, no alibis or words are needed to justify its presence. You feel it. You just feel it. As if it were the wind on your skin. Through the hair. Without being forever, because it never stopped being forever. The truth is that love never has a beginning. Nor an end. You recognise it. Once more. Beyond all death. Beyond all life.

The selfish person is not the one who wants everything for themselves, but the one who does not care what others want. They're the ones who seem to be waiting when in fact they have already left. They are always the first to disappear the moment they start to be recognised. Their need to appear impartial is only comparable to their cowardice. They run away without letting their escape be noticed. It is the art of leaving the tears for those who stay. The wound for those who fall. The promise for those who are left without the dream. The pain for those who love them.

I educate my children to be free. I never talk to them about failures or mishaps, but about responsibility and choices. I like to make them smile at everything, because even sadness brings a joy that few know. I don't want them to be like me. My greatest ambition is to let them choose what they want. They will perhaps learn the hard way. Or not. It doesn't matter. The important thing is that they learn for themselves. That they feel the pain. That they feel the love. That they feel everything with the certainty that life is made of opposites. There is what remains. There is what leaves. And still what marks.

The day I realised that my father's words no longer affected me, I felt sorry for him, not the kind of pity that can be confused with compassion, but the kind that makes me sad. The truth is that I saw him for the first time with the eyes of one who has stopped believing in a man who deep down never existed. It was as if I myself had become aware that I had become an adult and was no longer the little boy in love with his lifelong hero. I didn't stop loving him, but I realised that my love for him was made of far more mysterious things than I ever imagined possible. I loved my father like someone who loves a part of themselves that no longer exists. I loved him because I never knew how not to love him. I loved him because he taught me not to be like him. As simple as that. Like a path without stars, but still full of moonlight.

I've never been able to hate anyone. I've rebelled and threatened. I've even grabbed collars. But I don't know how to hate, even if I really want to. What I do with people who disrespect me is to be indifferent. Indifference is my natural way of showing the hatred I can't feel.

I need to put my head against a chest that breathes calm and asks nothing of me. I don't want anything else. That's all. I want to receive a hug that envelops me like a snuggle without any words mixed in. I am often in need of silence. To invent new silences. Those that can replace the ones I know. Capable of calming what I think. What I feel. Silences that take me back to nothingness. Only to the quiet embrace of the one I sought the chest to rest. Someone who knows me without needing to understand me. Who loves me without needing to undress me. Who survives the lack of me when I leave again. At dawn. Without speaking except with their eyes. As I've always done since I became free.

There are things I can't change. Nor do I want to. They are things I love, things that make me who I am. With each time I live, I bring some more into my life and let others go. The ones that leave, no longer need to stay. Those that come in, bring me new smiles and unknown sensations. The truth is that I have never believed in the repeatable. I maintain that everything is always done differently, even though it may seem identical. If everything were the same, nothing would change and everything would seem more of the same. Life would be an absence of that which I would never know if I would ever need. Love would be like a leap between what I would like to have lived and what would never have happened to me. I would be someone threatened by that which I never feared. A mixture of fear and what I don't seek. A person without a soul wanting to write.

I will keep trying until I fail better. I'm going to take risks until I feel brave enough to no longer feel like giving up. I'm going to leave to never let myself stay. I'll leave as often as I need to until I don't want to come back. I will follow unknown paths to live stories never imagined. I will cry so that I never unlearn to do it. I will laugh until I find a place where I am not forbidden to laugh. It doesn't matter how, or for how long. The important thing is to keep doing what was once impossible and has now become novelty.

I lose myself in smiles when I see a woman in love. I am touched by the delicate way she shakes her shoulders as she approaches. A woman in love offers the best of herself without emptying herself. She knows better than anyone else the times when the verb to love can be conjugated and offered. She does not love in order to be loved. She loves because she believes in her very own way of feeling love. She loves because she cannot lie to herself. If she did, love would no longer be to define what she feels, but rather to show what she refused not to feel. A woman in love is first and foremost a woman. She is someone for whom love is the reason for staying even closer to herself.

A woman's worst failing is to think she can change me. I only change something about myself if I feel it makes sense to change. I have learned to be a loner and to choose only what smells like me and speaks my language. I love the woman who allows me to be myself. I love the woman who doesn't demand from me what I can't give. I love being generous with those who understand me. I ask for nothing and accept everything that is given to me with love. Only with love, because only love transforms me. Transforms one and the other. Like a smile or a kiss given at the right moment. That's all.

Everything that you repeat over and over again becomes a truth for you. From then on, your whole attitude is affected by what you have come to believe. There is no point in doubting, because you have already surrendered to a power greater than you know. When I understood this tendency of the human being, I began to find no more excuses to question everything I believed in. Without much effort, I discovered pretensions of normality in many of my choices. I easily understood why my life kept resembling a dance without music, a tap dance performed by bare feet. Deep down, I didn't want to change anything. I had become a stamp of fear stuck on a letter never sent. A repetition kept with the conviction of being a novelty. A cursing time, but still the only one I accepted to live. This is how a stupid person is formed. Nothing in him is improvisation. Everything in him boils down to microscopes and magnifying glasses used to see only what he allows himself to see.

I'd rather make mistakes than get it right. I've always linked my mistakes to a life certificate. If I never make a mistake, I'll never know what it's like to laugh at myself. It annoys me that I have to get it right, when getting it right means for me to reach the end. When I get it wrong, I keep on living. I keep wanting to go somewhere, even though I don't even know how I'm going to get there. In fact, I just want to be here. To live everything and a lot. To err endlessly and let myself stay in the error, because only those who know how to err also know how to get it right.

My destiny is to write until I die. It is my addiction. My blood transfusion. It's a kind of journey I don't wish to stop taking for anything in this world. Not even if I die alone clutching sheets of paper and pens almost out of ink. Not even if there is no longer an audience. Because I always write for me. For no one else. I would never know how to write for others. I would get the impression that I was passing between raindrops and yet getting all wet. From head to toe. As if in a weeping without eyes. As if it was a strange form of life without a path of its own. A death devoid of any morals. Of any sense.

I love the language of trees and the way they tell me that there is no point in putting down roots. They whisper in my ear that everything has another logic so different from the one we think we know. They shout at me to leave, not to stay always in the same place doing the same thing. They tell me that after a while the wind becomes painful. They remind me that the beauty of things is not in their colour but in their movement. Everything that moves without leaving its place is half dead inside. It lacks the freedom to start stories and walk trails without looking back. They tell me that the only thing that matters is being able to fly without wings. To leave without a destination. To die with a smile on your lips. Just like when we were born.

Among many truths and some secrets, I smile when someone reads what I have not written and accuses me of being who I am not. Anyone can interpret what they want about what I write. Anybody at all. I will not change a line of what I wrote, nor a thought of what I feel. I live today, because only today exists. Tomorrow will be whatever I choose to follow. That's it and nothing else. I am a dreamer. That's true. But a dreamer of today. Someone who wants to live each day intensely as if it were a dream. Just a dream. An endless dream. Full of many other dreams. Just like me.

If we knew a little more about love, perhaps we would need to love even more in order to feel it. If we understood love more, we would probably find that pain is the only way to love. If we were not so stupid, perhaps we would not run away from love so much and would live more without looking for it. Love does not go through any of this. Love reveals itself only in what it makes you feel. Everything else exists because you don't feel it. It exists only because you believe you feel it.

The need to protect ourselves always comes from the fear of being exposed. There is in each of us a lack of courage in the permanent will to defend ourselves from what we believe is threatening us. We are afraid to face almost anything, even when our life depends on it. We face things always believing in the existence of miracles, which is the same as saying that we do not believe in ourselves. Tolerating the intolerable makes us into who we are not. It makes us who we think it is best to be. In the name of protection without a net or a floor. In the name of a security that takes our lives. In the name of a bunch of things we don't even bother to give a name to anymore.

Love never has a beginning. Not even when it is for the first time. Love is love before it even happens. You recognise it. Just because it is love. That's all. And nothing else.

I feel closer and closer to you. Not far away, not near. Just closer to being with you. To be in you. To be part of you. Forever. Like a tattoo under the skin. A tattoo that only you know exists. Like a secret. Or a longing. A longing for what I haven't lived yet. A longing that brings me even closer to you, because when I imagine myself near you, I feel even closer to me. Just like that, so simple. Like a love made only of love.

My truth never makes me dependent on anything or anyone. It is a journey without time or distance to the centre of my heart. It is a path I only want to travel with hands in my pockets and smile on my face. I learned long ago that speaking the truth is the best way to avoid the usurpation of the soul. Or forgetting it. Or the deviation of what we don't want to stop feeling as our own. Never. Never again.

One day I will die, as surely as one day I was born. Of my birth I remember nothing. Of my death I am not at all sure how it will happen. I hope that my time here will still be long. I want to do many things before I lose the ability to believe in them and eventually stop feeling them. Old age doesn't scare me, but dementia is a fatality of many poets and writers. Writing without feeling must resemble breathing while sleeping. It only serves to stay alive with no notion that one is alive. A strange combination of life and death, of light and darkness. As I believe to be the moment when I will close my eyes for the last time. The return to a dream where I no longer risk being awakened. The victory of who never accepted to enter any race.

The ability to produce diversity is the secret to knowing how to live better. When we exist only in routine and sameness, in meaningless habits and in meaningless stops, more of the same becomes our island with no way out. We learn to live with what we are afraid of losing, as if losing would mean dying. Or worse. As if to lose was to suffer from an incurable disease. The absence of diversity in life creates a lack of immunity to suffering. We start to live without a single smile, as if smiling had become our greatest impossibility. The truth is that without new paths, words and times, life runs away from the unforgettable and leaves us lost between almost nothing and what never was. And what probably never will be.

What defines you is what you do with yourself. It's not what you think, or what you believe, or even what you feel. It is what you do with yourself, because that is what reflects who you are actually being at your innermost core. There is a conflict within you. A lack of coherence between your inside and your outside. It happens, but it shouldn't. If you want to change what you do, do it all from your truth and not from the truth of others. The truth of others is your greatest illusion. It is what turns you into something you are not. It turns you into a lie camouflaged by greater lies. Someone who looks at himself without ever recognizing himself.

Accepting the love of others for us is a difficult matter when we do not love ourselves. It should be the other way round, but we can't do it any differently. Mistrust does not allow us to separate our emotions and live one without the other. Loving ourselves is above all the attitude of accepting ourselves and not others. Those who do not love themselves find it difficult to believe in someone's love for them, simply because they believe that they can only give back to them what they give to themselves. The truth is that loving ourselves can never be something half-hearted. It has to be total surrender in an endless disengagement with ourselves. A desert of a single oasis. A flight with a sure fall, but also the only way of offering ourselves that which never ceased to belong to us.

I have long argued that nothing has an end, but rather a transformation that began long ago. Whoever says something is over wants to believe that it is easy to turn pages without opening a book. Nothing has an end, because every ending is always the beginning of something in some way related to the previous one. What happens once, does not happen again in the same way. It happens in the effect of the first one. If it didn't, we were just unconnected moments, quick successive stories without any link. But the truth is quite different. We are the sum of stories joined together, where each one carries a bit of our new change. What I do today, always reflects a part of who I was, even if in an indelible and almost imperceptible way. If I am attentive, I will feel it in the smallest details. If not in my attitude, it is in some sad repetition of myself. The truth is that, no matter how much I don't want to, there will always be parts of who I am that will never be different. There is nothing to do. Nor to undo. Just accept it.

The greatest secret of life is that it has no secret. We may not know it very well, but it is not because it remains hidden. It is only because we have not yet managed to understand it in its entirety. Also if this were to happen, it is because the time has come for us to leave for other dimensions and spaces. But this is not yet possible. What we should do is to look for the inspiration to live our own life. Without secrets. Only with discoveries and without guilt. As if we composed a song or wrote a book. As if we spoke only through smiles. As if we always treated each other as souls.

The most difficult moment is the one when you have to decide whether to stay in it or to leave in search of other moments. The search for a new moment cannot be mere survival. Most of us search without finding what we don't even know we are looking for. We wander through life to be found by what we are not even looking for. Pure deceit. Whatever we find, we attract so that we can change our sensitivities. If we are not sensitive, the worst they can ask of us is to leave a moment. Only the sensitive can look for another moment without the feeling that they are missing something. They know they deserve it. They know the beginning of each one and love to ignore the script. They would rather fly than stay on the ground.

I like people who don't just write words. Words often sound just like words. They are written more and more without feeling. They write because they say that writing changes what is the same in us. I believe more that writing makes us enter a world where only those who feel remain. Who does not feel, does not write. They put words together. They try to give them life. As if it were possible to give birth to words without any pain.

I have an angel with no name next to me. The truth is he doesn't need a name. I don't see any wings or white robes either. In fact, I never see anything. I just feel it. Like a touch or a breath close to my ear. In the smallest smile that he puts on my lips. In the voice that makes me listen inside my heart. Without being able to be different from what it is. No more and no less than you are being. My angel without a name. Just and so much.

One of these days, I'm going to get on a plane and fly to where I've never been before. I feel like living what life is inviting me to live. I believe that if I don't dare to follow what I feel, I will never know why I am here. I don't want to wait any longer. I do not wish to give up on understanding anything I know I have come to live. Life is not in my ability to live it, but in my ability to feel it. It exists to be felt in the way that has the most to do with me. My way. Only mine. The same way that will be with me when I climb the stairs of the plane. When I travel the skies and seas. When I reach the place where I have been waiting for more than an eternity.

Stop wanting to control. Forget any and all expectations. Don't wait for results and consequences. Do not choose to remain still or stand still. It is of no use to you because you are always waiting for something that is not yet with you and may never be. You are here to live in the moment without thinking about anything else. Live each instant intensely without wanting to know how it will be afterwards. Live everything that your heart asks you to live. Perhaps you do not yet know, but if you do not follow your heart, you will never understand what you are doing here. You will always want to find something that you can perpetuate in your life when the important thing is just to live what you are living. If you don't like it, change it. If you don't like it, leave. If you don't like it, pick something new. But live. Live everything as if it were always the first time. Only in this way will you make your soul evolve and not that of others.

Giving up deep parts of ourselves cannot be part of who we are. Only those who stop believing give up. To give up on ourselves is to not believe in what we are capable of being as the owners of our skin and of our soul. To give up is to stop believing in our courage to create what is made for us and to prefer to do nothing but make excuses and senseless arguments. Life is not a tyranny from which we must flee, because fleeing has the same smell as giving up. It smells of endless fear, an odour of a lack of bravery, a perfume that smells of nothing. We were made to invade ourselves with inspiration and walk a path offered to us at every step by a life eager for us. We were made to live as if each day brings us even more life, even more time to choose what we are passionate about. To give up who we are is tantamount to saying that life doesn't need what we can give it. That which only belongs to us from the moment we share it with someone.

Accept what you are living now so that one day you can access what you cannot even imagine being able to live. When you accept, you take responsibility for what is yours. Nothing in life is exempt from responsibility. Everything exists for a reason. Your life is the result of your choices, whether they are fear or love for you. Nothing escapes self-forgetfulness if it is not remembered by yourself. It is like a memory or a photograph. When you accept a memory, you give it life, you make it ever-present. When you review a photograph, you remember the smells and the words spoken. To accept something is not to submit. Quite the contrary. It is to be able to change it without dying beforehand.

No emptiness is filled with dependence. When you choose to depend on someone or something to give meaning to your life, you are like a stage without actors, a monologue without an audience, a miserable person lost in the middle of a crowd you think you know. It is easy to offer the benefit of the doubt to a liar, but it is very difficult to get out of the illusion of your lies. You will only understand your emptiness when you don't need anyone to explain it to you. Only when you allow yourself to truly feel the pain it causes you, its enormity, its bitter intimacy with you, will you understand its reasons. There are no voids without dependencies. Understand what you depend on and free yourself. Let go of what ties you to a place where you no longer wish to stay. Leave without a destination. Be guided by what life tells you to choose. Without fear or with fear. Whatever. Draw from your emptiness the willingness to live the most genuine of truths, the one you don't even know exists within you. Embrace the time that is beginning to escape you. Make your life an undiscovered word.

You have to learn to quiet your mind, to be still, to become aware of what is around you and what is not on your side. You have to learn to allow yourself to feel each of the emotions that you experience when you look at each of the things around you. Do not think about anything. Feel only, but only the light side of everything. Do not let the heavy side of each thing interfere with your feeling, for this will cause you to experience fear. Remember that fear comes from your mind and is fed to you so that you are even more afraid to feel. It is only when you feel that you are aware of your own nature. When you think, you run away from it, just as you insist on running away whenever you experience pain or suffering. You have to learn to calm your mind so that you understand who you truly are. You have to learn to calm your mind so that you do not blame anyone for the life you live and so that you can solve your problems without ever ceasing to be yourself.

Whether you like it or not, you are always creating. Creation is a process that is natural to you from the moment you are born. The difference lies in what you decide to think about, because every thought is a creation. Nothing happens by chance, especially if you create this chance yourself. The solution lies in not having judgemental thoughts about anything or anyone. When you do not judge, you change your whole life. When you do not judge, you begin to feel gratitude for everything that happens to you, even the most difficult and painful things. When you accept what happens to you, you are conceiving the possibility of creating its opposite through your choices. Remember that only the existence of opposites gives you the chance to choose different opportunities. Remember that only in the presence of darkness can you see the light. Simple, just like that. Like the air that exists without you seeing it or the moment that arises without you expecting it.

You have to stop being afraid of losing that which makes you suffer. Where there is a will, there will always be a way. If something makes you suffer, it is certainly not helping you to find your peace. Suffering is the most painful way of choosing to live. It is only in your life because you have decided to let it stay, because you are afraid of what you can live without it. You were led to believe that suffering is the most noble way of being in life, especially if you suffer for others. You have been deliberately deceived in order to take away your capacity to see the wonder of who you are and not to have the capacity to believe in yourself. When you choose to stay in suffering, nothing changes. Quite the contrary. It only gets worse. Decide how you are going to feel about suffering, instead of letting suffering decide how you are going to feel. If you succeed, your whole life will take on the meaning that you want to give it. You are free to live the greatest adventure of your existence. You finally understand that you only find yourself when you stop suffering.

Even if you don't want it, there are things you'll have to go through in life. What will make the difference is how you accept and live them. You can live them in the middle ground, you can run away from them or face them because you attracted them, even though you don't want them. Some are pleasant and others require you to be more than who you think you are. They are the ones that teach you to surrender to yourself in order to offer yourself your best. They are the ones that show you what you have to do with yourself and your life, that show you a different path or drag you to the same place where you insist on staying. It all depends solely on you, on your will to open a new cycle or to stay forever in a time that smells of mould and suffering. On you and nobody else. Only you.

I have loved people and lost them without being able to do anything to stop it. Life has this generous side of not always giving us what we so much desire. I have loved people and let them go without being able to break the silence of their departure. I allowed them to go away without admitting that I preferred them to stay, as if my greatest weakness lay in a proudly unspoken word that would make them turn their heads back in my direction. I have loved people and not had the courage to tell them how much I loved them. I kept silent as if I did not know how to use my lips or was afraid to say what they might not want to hear. I loved people and lied to them because I was afraid of suffering. I ran away from each one of them because I was not bold enough to be crazy enough to want to live a love without fear that it might end. I loved people like I never knew how to love myself and I didn't want to accept that I would never be without any part of what made me myself if I lived those loves. I have loved people and I know that I will never stop loving, not because it is easy to love, but because if I stop loving I will stop breathing, I will wither as if I had been forgotten to be watered. I'll die hugging myself, alone and in silence, like someone who has become a black angel condemned never to be able to spread their wings again. Just like that. Just like this. For time on end. In the memory of everything I was afraid to live.

One does not love someone without torment, because love also lives from its opposite. There is always mystery in everything that one does not understand. There is always a hidden desire for everything one runs away from, a secret, tumultuous desire, like a poison without an antidote, a dialogue of those who listen only to what suits them. To love is not only to love. It's also smiling at the least appropriate moment, it's kissing from afar with your fingertips, it's fearlessly touching the scar you made when you left without looking back. To love is more than just to love. It's knowing what not even the other knows about themselves. It's crying and laughing in the refusal of our miserable condition of being in love with the fear of not knowing how to love. It's staying, even when the pain tells you to leave. It's tearing the skin once and for all so that there is no possible cure. It is to live as if death were always the beginning of what one believes will never come to an end.

Having someone with whom to share what hurts is like resting your heart inside your soul. To have someone with whom you can cuddle up, in silence, without being asked anything, without trying to provoke what you don't want to say, is to live an instant with the scent of life. To have someone who moves your hair with the same quietness of a caress and of a shelter, someone who gives you back a smile where before there were only lips compressed by unspoken words, it is to be saved from the madness of becoming nobody. Love is also made of all this, of silences, of spaces generously granted, of refuges made to measure our pain, of swims that work as if everything could be. To have someone with whom to share our imperfections is to become similar in our differences, it is to be able to add and subtract without needing to have any notion of mathematics or geometry, it is to know how to distinguish what is from what can never be, it is to understand all the beauty of waking up in the middle of the night just to look at the serene sleep of the one sleeping next to us.

If we could guess who we have in front of us, it would be much easier to know who is lying to us. I have learnt with time to recognise the traits of those who tell me lies. The truth is that whoever lies, always smiles, whether it's with their lips, their eyes, their shoulders or their hands. A smile doesn't have to be visible. There are smiles that we neither see nor feel. They have the ability to hide behind words and promises. However, if we are attentive, we see them without even having to open our eyes. We feel them creeping up our skin, slowly, almost imperceptible, like the warmth of another skin approaching ours in the gentleness of a bed where we no longer want to be. Lies are like smiles shot at close range. They almost always kill us without us noticing them.

My eyes are not the eyes of sadness. They are the eyes of those who have learned a lot through sadness. They are the eyes of one who understands sadness. In truth, I wouldn't be who I am if I hadn't been someone who was sad so many times, because only sadness had the capacity to transform me into someone capable of living in peace with myself. I no longer believe in suffering because it no longer answers the questions I most wanted answered. I began to believe in myself. I have come to believe in the beauty that sadness has entrusted me.

There are people we should not let be part of our lives. We have no obligation to put up with them, nor to allow them to impose themselves on our choices. We let them do so because we are afraid of not knowing how to live without them or of displeasing them. Life is a unique experience. Life is to be decided by us and nobody else. When we give that power to others, we take away all the natural colours from our dreams and start living only what they let us live. All that is always very little or almost nothing. It is suffering for the stupidity of not knowing how to exist in any other way. It is to kneel before a deaf and blind god. It is handing over our lives to those who constantly push us away from their memory.

Never worry about what you know or what you don't know. In fact, never worry about anything. Worry is a waste of time, a useless suffering, a lament only said to be heard. Those who worry wish to change something they know nothing about. It is a kind of indecipherable joke that is taken too seriously. As if it was a failure or a condemnation. It is better to accept what happens without confusing acceptance with submission. They are completely different things. To accept is to stop and then choose what has to do with us. To submit is to want to put together what is indivisible. It means finding a problem where there is only life.

Never stop someone from leaving. Let your wound heal itself. It was you who created it in the times when you preferred to complicate what was simple. Perhaps you have learned something from the pain you feel. Or not. Life is a reflection of what you give yourself and not to others. If that was the case, many of us would just be a consent without consequence. Next time, take care of yourself before you tell someone you love them. Tell them the truth. Tell them you need them and you want them to make you happy.

Maybe they'll understand. Maybe they will tell you that they are not there to make you happy, but to show you the way to your happiness. Maybe they won't even tell you anything. Perhaps they will leave before saying a word because they understand that you will make them suffer. Perhaps they will leave because they understand before you that you understand nothing of how to love someone without giving up loving yourself too.

It is difficult for you to understand what you are afraid of. You prefer to run away or to attack. You are capable of anything, except asking yourself why you are afraid. Maybe if you looked for an answer you would come out stronger. Perhaps you would stop living between desires and unfulfilled promises, between silences and words stupidly kept on the tip of your tongue. Fear is what you need to understand in order to move forward. It is the demon you have to excommunicate. It is the angel that hides beneath your lack of courage eager to be set free. Or maybe not. Maybe you prefer fear because it gives you the excuse to stay in the same place, the safe conduct to justify your cowardice, the opportunity to change nothing. Eventually even the reason to kill hope with a clear shot between the eyes.

Life is only worth living if we are crazy about it, if we are ready to die to continue living. When we live without loving life, we live as if we were dead. Nothing matters more than enough to keep pestering us. Everything stays only as long as it takes to leave without a trace or mark on our skin. Every thing is a repetition of ourselves without being aware of who we are. Only those who love life can go crazy to the point of understanding that it is life that makes us both wonderful and insane, because most of us will not be remembered for what we have done but for what we have lived. We don't know what happens between lives. We only know that we are alive. We understand what few understand. We recognise what almost nobody sees. We live fragments of moments that last for eternities. We love life, not because it loves us, but because to live without loving it is the same as choosing to lie when one desperately wants to speak the truth.

You don't forget who you love, but you also don't forget who makes you suffer. But those who make you suffer don't love. Or don't know how to love, which is probably the same thing, because making someone suffer is anything but love. Perhaps it is the most faithful representation of human stupidity, the perfect copy of the imbecility of the human being. To love is to be able to breathe through the other's skin. It's being certain of what you didn't know you knew. It's flying without leaving the place, as if instead of wings you had a corner where the other person could put his or her face. The love I know is different from everything else because it is not only mine. It also belongs to the person who makes me feel it, because he who loves knows that there is nothing else that is his alone. Even if you want it very much. Because to love is also not wanting what you had all by yourself. It's having a name that was written in the sum of two smiles.

A sad soul is a soul lined with mourning. It is a soul almost departed. It is a soul that has failed to exist with joy. With enthusiasm. With life. It is a soul that was never felt by the one it chose to live the greatest love of all. It was ignored. Not listened to. Forced to remain in the deepest darkness of a body. Prevented from offering the best of herself. Reduced to the silence of a death foretold. Of a procession of demons. Of a cry of angels. Of a condemnation without forgiveness. A sad soul is like a sun hiding under its own shadow. Just so. So little of nothing and nothing of so much that could have been.

Every day I keep my conscience awake so that I don't let myself fall into the temptation of choosing the easiest instead of the best for me. Life asks this of us so that we can fully live it. We easily fall into the stupidity of feeling sorry for ourselves, lying to ourselves or excusing ourselves for allowing disrespect in our lives. Surviving is easy. Living asks us to be vigilant. It is as simple as that. Especially when times are painful and costly to bear. In difficult times, we must listen only to our truth, the one that lives inside our hearts, far from everything that separates good from evil, far from what makes us decide without wanting to think about the answers or be attentive to the signs. Life exists in each one of us. Unfortunately, few live it without forgetting themselves.

When change calls you, don't resist it. To resist change is to resist life. It is choosing to continue in suffering. Your change calls out to you, as someone who knows what in that moment is best for who you have chosen to be. You can listen to it or not. Everything depends only on your will and determination to face your greatest fears. To accept life is to give it the chance to head in your direction. Do not let it slip through your fingers. Do not condemn it to death. Remember that you are more than what a mirror reflects. You are someone who has been given a name. You are someone who has been given a life to live. Don't waste it being who you never wanted to be. Slam your fist down on the table. Scream a scream unlike any other. And let go of the hell you've created without wanting it.

Only the determined find a way. The others live accidentally. Only the daring live life. The rest live only what they are allowed to live. Only those who speak the truth know themselves beyond all lies. Liars suffer in silence the consequences of their words. Nothing in life happens by chance. Everything lies in the ability of those who understand why we are here. And even if there is no reason, there is a story to live. For each one of us. All different. All precious. Lives even greater than you can imagine. Lives present far beyond what one insists on not living.

At this moment when you speak ill of your life, many would love to live it for you. When I accompanied my father in his terminal phase, I knew suffering from an angle that I had never witnessed before in my life. Every face that crossed our paths in the corridors of the Portuguese Institute of Oncology, every look from those who sat next to us in the waiting rooms, every groan at cost muffled between my hands or against a handkerchief taped to my mouth, let me see how far someone's anguish and pain can go. Right now when you're complaining about your life, you should rethink every one of your thoughts and give thanks to life for what is being given to you. There is another world that many of us do not know about. A world apart where nothing is certain or predictable. A place where the soul often loses hope and its compass. A place you should visit so that, when you leave, you give more priority to everything you don't value because you don't lack it yet.

Your skin has a softness that only I know, a smell of roses gagged in your name, a colour that has been tinted on purpose to blind me. I love to touch it lightly with my fingertips, with the outline of my lips, to travel along it like an endless path, to offer it what I have never felt with anyone else. I love kissing it with the same ardour with which I lock it to contain the desire that I put off with more and more difficulty. I love to hold you tightly when I pull you to me, when I become eternal in your touch, when I swear to love you forever, when I make you mine without you ceasing to be yours. Your skin becomes even more beautiful, sweaty, trembling, shining on that body of yours of a satiated woman, female without reins, indomitable animal, empress of my kingdom. One day, when the world is no longer the world, I shall make you eternal with a dance, but not just any dance. A dance where life will be unable to die.

A stubborn child is not a child who wants attention. It is a child who feels his parents' suffering. Stubbornness is their own way of expressing the guilt they feel when they feel them suffering. Most parents cannot imagine the impact that their emotions and feelings have on their children. They may pretend that everything is fine, but children don't need words to understand. Not even forced smiles or consoling hugs. Nothing goes unnoticed because they have the ability to see without opening their eyes, to listen to what they are not even told. Stubbornness is the only way they know to manifest all their impotence in solving what they believe they are causing. For a child, everything the parents manifest is because of them. In other words. They are always the guilty ones, the burning witches, the ones responsible for the pain they cause to those they love the most. Sad fate when they are not understood, when instead of solving they only make it worse. They can only continue. Perhaps the day will come when someone will understand the reason for their stubbornness, or else let it turn into a hopeless rebellion, a poison for life.

Living with someone you don't love is like living in the land of the dead. Every homecoming gets lost along the way, lost in destination and identity. Smiles are like shrugging shoulders and kisses have become with the years a quick touch with a taste of warm wax. Nothing else tastes the same, to what was lived when you still believed it could be love. Only love is a place you never want to leave, a life that lasts beyond life, not a place where indifference and routine gain pus. A gangrene without amputation. A life sentence served with your eyes closed. To live with someone you don't love is to die in an endless exile. It is to kill the other with a shot at oneself.

I'm not a loner, but I don't love crowds either. I enjoy being with myself, just as I find pleasure in being with good friends. I'm not one for going to loud parties where everything is too fast and confusing. I prefer a good conversation with a generous wine, words that lose their lucidity as the bottle is emptied and laughter that solves thoughts already deprived of any instruction book. It is always important for me to feel at peace, even in the midst of all the disorder. I'm also not one to run away from conflict when it clashes with me, but I avoid it. I'm not one for routines, but I love habits, the kind that give a little more meaning to every day of my life in the same way that they ensure that I sometimes need to break them. I do it not out of stubbornness or even stupidity. Just because a carefully allowed unforeseen event always makes me gain a new friend or live a new adventure.

To stop being insecure is an impossibility because, in one way or another, at one time or another, we all have insecurities. Each day we live is unrepeatable. Each step we take can be both the last and the first towards a new path. Insecurity is part of the unpredictability of life. Security is an illusion we build to hide our fear of losing what we think is ours or of failing to live up to what is expected of us. I myself have moments when insecurity knocks on my window. I've known it for years. It's like an old friend who reminds me how much I still need to learn about myself and life. It is the bearer of the reminder that I am no more or better than anyone else. It is the messenger that keeps me from being arrogant or ridiculous to others.

Once in a while, leaving is the best solution. To start everything from scratch. Leaving empty-handed, free, without fear of what might happen the next day. Deep down, we all have this desire at least once in our lives. Let go of the routine and the suffering, the unhappiness and the frustration, slam the door and leave for good. To think of nothing, to hesitate for no second, to be happy, whatever that might be. But almost nobody does it and prefers to go on dreaming about what they insist on ignoring, about what they insist on doing nothing to change their non-existence. In truth, the vast majority of people are nothing but a bunch of cowards who have more fear in their veins than blood. What they don't know is that life begins beyond their fears. Beyond the mediocrity of always choosing the same sad way home. Beyond dying without having found what they never dared to look for.

People have not yet understood that the path is more important than the arrival. The path is life, what you choose each day without thinking too much about what you want to achieve. When you live thinking about the end, you usually get tired before your time, give up or find reasons to abandon what deep down you never wanted. To live is to choose for the pleasure of living. It's being crazy enough to understand that without life nothing is worth living. It is to give lightness to what before seemed too heavy. It is not being afraid of being afraid. It's always having a smile on your face because smiling is the gift of those who are not afraid to cry. Of those who are not afraid of sadness. Of those who have discovered the secret of slowness behind all haste.

Out of nowhere, everything changes. Life is generous to that extent. You may not even accept certain changes, but they happen because you need them to respect you or correct today something that you insist on wanting to stay the same. It is not an easy task. Sometimes it knocks you down like a dry blow on the head. Other times, it makes you cry and calls many things into question. There are even times when it almost drives you mad and makes you forget that the impossible exists so that one day you can make it possible. Life wants you to know your best, but you're too busy with what you're allowed and not with what has to do with you. It is a death you think you don't care about at all when in fact you are making it less worthy of you every day. You need the boldness of one who has nothing left to lose to conquer what belongs to you, what belongs to that soul you carry and believe very little in itself. You are a kind of warrior tired of never having fought because you do not know that there is a battle to be fought. A madman without enough conscience to realize that he has immense sanity underneath all his madness. Someone who does not know or dream that ease is the friend of smallness, of mediocrity. Of all that you will never live or risk giving your life to if you don't fill the present with a lot of freedom.

I like people who dare to dress their difference without fear of being stripped naked by the judgement of others. There is in them a rebelliousness made of passion, the same passion that makes them free without fear of being imprisoned. For a long time I have not understood those who waste their lives for fear of living them. Nor do I understand those who insist on being chameleons among the bushes of disloyalty to themselves. Not living is the same as sleeping awake. There comes a time when sleep becomes a haunting from which one flees for fear of falling asleep forever. Of dying without believing that it is possible to dream. Of remaining in the deepest darkness believing one can see the light.

You should give more importance to your sadness. If you could read it, you would decipher life codes. Maybe even the secret of your eternity. But you are afraid of being sad. You're afraid that it will take away your ability to see what you think only joy can give you. Let me tell you that it is in sadness that you meet your most delicate side, the most fragile, the closest to you, the one that teaches you to accept that which you most run away from. When you are sad you give your soul hope of finding itself again, you gain a voice of your own that only it understands. Because only sadness has the power to make you aware of what you need to do to become happy again.

I like to be alone, not to escape from others, but to find myself. Every moment I experience, I have to share it afterwards in silence with myself. It's a kind of ritual that helps me to better understand my life. I am already a loner, not the kind who avoids people, but more the kind who only values what is worthy of being valued. I no longer have the patience to waste time with hypocrisy and meaningless conversations. When I socialise, I'm like a fish in water because I give of myself without reserve. I am no longer afraid of giving myself because I have learnt to feel to whom I can give myself. It is a talent I have developed by believing in what I feel. If it wasn't like this, I would suffer from disappointments. Today, nobody disappoints me anymore. I have learned not to expect anything from anyone. I realized that I am happier giving without fear of not receiving. I have become free because I want nothing from others but what they want to give me without my having to ask them once.

People want friends without understanding what friendship is. They believe that a few confidences and a few nights of laughter and parties are enough to have friends. A friendship is not a simple exchange of moments or words. If that were the case, there wouldn't be so much deception and betrayal between people. A friendship is like a true love. It lasts forever. It endures what you didn't even know existed. It endures beyond time and is an attribute that few have the privilege to experience, a connection more vivid than all answers without the need for questions, a place where memories smell like life. In truth, having a friend is so much more than having a friend. It is to know someone whose skin and soul are tattooed with your name, someone who offers you the best of themselves without asking for anything, someone whose absence makes themselves present without anything ever being the same, but as if everything were different each time.

Suffering is a choice. I know it is difficult to accept this statement, but those who choose suffering choose the easiest path. Feeling sorry for ourselves makes life easier because it excuses us from choosing a different path. It is frightening what we do to ourselves in the name of the cowardice of living. We prefer to stay in suffering rather than face it because the truth is that we always benefit from staying in it. It sounds crazy to say such a thing, but it is the truest of truths. Whoever chooses to remain in suffering allows himself to flee from what he is afraid of living. Those who stay in suffering take total responsibility for the conquest of their own life.

To have courage is not to do what everyone else can do. Having courage is not being afraid to face your own fears. Each person is different from everyone else, but the fears are basically the same. It is good to read, to listen, to learn, but the hardest thing is to put into practice what you read, listen and learn. You have to really want it. It is fundamental to believe that we are capable of understanding why we feel the fears in order to be able to face and overcome them. It is not for everyone. It is only for those who want to live their best life.

We live in different times, times that condemn us to live erratically or to value new possibilities. Chance is not part of life. If it was, everything would be more difficult. Nothing happens without an origin and without generating consequences. Whatever you did yesterday, condemns you or frees you today once again. We live in times of change, times that ask us to take ourselves more seriously than usual. We have been living accidentally for too long and without stopping to reconsider the wrong we do to ourselves each day. Whether we like it or not, these new times will definitely make us die inside or be reborn to no longer obediently accept a meaningless life.

Your life depends on the choices you make. Don't be angry with what you are living now. Accept it so that you can change. It doesn't matter what you complain about or who you blame. The important thing is what you decide. Don't give everything to God because He doesn't want so much responsibility. Do your part. Begin to see yourself instead of fleeing from your gaze. Look at yourself with eyes of silence. Contemplate your life as if you were judging someone else's. Understand and feel how you allow so much that you do not want, so much disrespect and offence, so many obligations and lies. Do not deceive yourself with promises or prayers, because these alone are not enough. Hold on to your life as you would hold on to the hand of the one you love and walk against that which hurts you and prevents you from being free. You have the power to choose the direction to take. Choose everything but that which takes you away from yourself. Choose to unveil secrets that not even you know. Begin to live the most forgotten side of your life. Heal within yourself that which you think is beyond remedy.

It is strange to think that one day we will take the place of our parents as the elders of the family. We will be missing something, as if childhood was suddenly extinguished once and for all, adolescence was nothing more than a distant time and adulthood was lost among scars, pains and quick memories of smiles, arrivals and departures. Burying one's parents is normal, but it puts us in a strange proximity with our own death. It is as if life whispers to us that we are next on the calendar of life. We then realise that we are now on our own, that there is no one else who can hold in our heads the idea that we are somehow still naively immortal. Our view of the world takes on a new dimension, a new angle, it gives us a greater understanding of our parents and their existence. For a reason that we will probably never understand, we feel responsible for what we are not responsible for. The children no longer need us, precisely because they still have us on their side. We, yes, we begin to want them closer, more present, only because they make us forget what we are afraid to remember, what haunts us as it must have haunted all those who came before us. Death has these things. It makes us want to live longer to let it remain in oblivion. In that place where the lack of remembrance is a talent.

I don't know if I'll ever see you again. I saw you without knowing I was going to see you and I saw you forever. I didn't see you more than in that instant, but I saw myself in seeing you. I saw you as if I saw eternity without any need for times or worlds. You didn't say a single word, but your eyes met mine and revealed to me what I never knew how to define or even feel. I saw what is similar in us, what enters our souls with the gentleness and vehemence of a life sentence lived in freedom. I saw myself and I saw myself again and again in the depth of your gaze, in the unexpected way you pierced my chest, in the way you gave my heart a name without knowing it. Then I saw you disappear with the same surprise with which I saw you emerge and I remained in silence, not in that silence that hurts, but in that silence that tells us that nothing will ever be the same again. A silence with the colour of life. A silence with the voice of an angel. A silence that only you will be able to inhabit again.

When you want to forget your past, you are only keeping it alive without realising its presence. The past is not to be forgotten, but rather accepted and understood, because otherwise it always comes back and much stronger than before. We can even create the illusion that we have left it behind only because we force ourselves not to think about it, but what is not understood comes back more and more determined to be part of the memory of those who want to kill it. Living the present without accepting the past is the same as wishing to love without having a heart. Nothing happens. Nothing changes. Everything is made of the same, even if it doesn't seem so, because the instant they force us to open our eyes, the first image that springs to mind is its memory. The past is not a disease. It is the medicine to cure the present. It is the trail to follow before the path. It is that ticket to the best film of our lives that we are afraid to buy, not because the plot is bad, but because we are afraid that the hero will end up dead at the end.

If you run away from yourself, you run away from your life. There is no way it can be otherwise, because life is you. When you run away from yourself, you get closer to everything that has nothing to do with you. You force yourself to breathe an air that asphyxiates you without taking your breath away. It weakens you like a word spoken in the middle of torture, at the moment when you think you are safe from your greatest enemy. Whether you like it or not, you are life, you are the cry you have not yet let out, the freedom you do not believe in. When you run away from yourself and mix with others, you hope to believe that you are like them, you want to resemble their mediocrity and frustration, their way of escaping from what is really important to live. But none of that works, nor does it save you from the suffering of not being yourself. It only makes you drunk for a time too short to be able to taste the texture of the real wine, the one that was supposed to give you enough clarity to understand that when you run away from yourself, you turn all your possibilities into impossibilities. You turn your heaven into a hell where you condemn yourself to be the only and last demon condemned to die without ever having lived what was uselessly left waiting for it.

It is not age that limits you, but the idea you have of yourself. Age is a time without windows or doors. It's a huge doorway that you insist on destroying or blocking up. To live is to be ageless. It means enjoying every moment as if they were steps on a staircase that takes you to where you have never been and never imagine going. You need to stop thinking about limits, stop believing in impossibilities. You must seize every moment of every day, photograph every instant so that it remains in the memory of what you don't need to remember. You must venture beyond every minute, every hour, cross the sound barrier only to understand that you can be a rocket ship ready to cross worlds and universes. I will tell you once again. You are not old. You have a life to live.

Never apologise when you want to ask a new question. Ask it and wait for the answer, not only because it might calm you down, but also because every answer reveals a thousand thoughts. Apologising out of fear is the same as existing without hope of living. The words come out of your mouth like cold cloths over an open wound and do not heal the pain in your soul. Quite the contrary. They make you scream inside what your lips would rather have said outside. And that kills you. It reduces you to someone who has lost a piece of life, someone who has let slip the opportunity to make a meaningful story out of his truth.

You have to find yourself before you give up looking for yourself. You are the most important person in your life. To give up on you is to wear a disguise every day to run away from what you fear. You weren't taught to see yourself. You were taught to look at yourself through the eyes of others. You believe you are who they say you are and act on that lie made true. You have to stop being afraid of who you are in the sadness and frustration of not living the life you were meant to be living. When you accept your sadness and frustration, you can finally understand what you are running away from. You can feel yourself beyond what your fingers feel when you touch yourself without being aware that you are doing so. You are more than skin and thoughts. You are the beginning of everything. It is in you that everything begins. Life. Truth. The purpose. The story you have yet to write.

I no longer fear what I used to fear. I already dare to go where before I didn't even dare to think of going. I already experience things I once did not even know. I already feel life much more than I ever did, not because it has changed with me, but rather because I have started to see it as I never saw it before. What in the past confused me, today delights me. What I used to run away from, now embraces me. I stopped asking it questions and started hearing answers where before there was silence. I no longer want to grab it in a hurry. I have understood that it only adjusts to me when my rhythm is identical to its own. Maybe not the way I want, but always the way I need. Like when it shows me that it really loves me. Like when it gets sad and at the same time smiles for the same reason. So its way. So my way. Like lovers. Life and I. Expecting nothing more than what we promised each other when we first met. A long time ago. Perhaps when neither of us knew yet the extent of the love that unites us. Or didn't even imagine that to love is simply to agree to stay.

Waking up alone in a strange city is one of the most pleasant sensations in life. It's like having adventure knocking at your bedroom door. We don't want to put our watch on our wrist so that the time doesn't limit our steps, nor do we want to know the names of the streets so that everything sounds unexpected. The joy with which we take to the city has no equal. Nothing stops us from smiling and welcoming every corner as the beginning of a new life. The pulsation of our veins sets the rhythm and reminds us how it feels to be young and bold again. Nothing frightens us, not even nightfall and the silence of the stars on the rooftops. There's always something about strange cities that reminds us of adolescence. It's not because of age. It is rather the surprise of being able to forget what year it is and the certainty that we cannot be happy if we run away from life.

If you experience a loss in your life without understanding it, you will continue to experience very similar losses until you understand why you have been attracting them. It seems a cruel way for life to warn you, but it knows no other way. If you don't understand at first, it will insist as many times as necessary until you understand what it is trying to tell you. Losses happen because you are not sufficiently aware of what you are doing. When you understand, you can finally change course and choose new paths and directions. The truth is that nothing will ever be the same again. Not even your biggest lies, because they will no longer be lies. They will only be memories of losses that you will no longer have to live through again.

My father was always my hero, even when I understood that I didn't want to be like him. Our heroes teach us everything we are supposed to learn, even what they themselves cannot demonstrate. A hero does not necessarily have to be a role model. Sometimes he is much more than a role model. He is the one who also shows you what you should do differently from him. That is the secret of many heroes. They teach what even they don't know. Just like my father with me. Because teaching is much more than knowing. To teach is to love.

It may sound crazy, but I like to sit still and wait for life to present itself to me. I like not doing anything other than what I feel like doing at every moment and not caring about anything else. I love not thinking about what is going to happen and not wanting to control my life. I feel free when I have no expectations. I know I don't know anything that I'm not supposed to know yet. I also don't want to know things out of time. I prefer to enjoy every moment of life. To be grateful for what I'm feeling. Just. Just. Because I also know that everything else will come on its own. In its time. In my time. Not to make me wait for what I don't need to wait for.

I never wanted a house of my own, because I never believed that I would stay in the same place forever. I've lived in different countries and cities, I've lived in many houses and flats, but I've never seen one as definitive. My Sagittarian side is too restless to want to see the sun rise on the same side all the time. I need to change landscapes and paths, angles and textures, lands and waters, stars and constellations, worlds and universes, but never loves. Not even for shadows. I have always been a man of one love. It is my story. It is my way of saying thank you to my heaven.

To be free is not to do everything you want. It is to do only what concerns us. Freedom is above all a choice. We can be free in the hardest and most demanding places. All we have to do is choose the good side of each thing over its better side. Everything in life has a good side, which is not always its better side, but is always the one that has more to do with us. To be free is to live the good side of everything, because it is that which communes directly with our soul. All freedom comes from the soul. All freedom only manifests itself when we live through our light. Never in any other way. Never in any other way.

Sometimes I think about myself as a teenager and I remember that my main characteristic was being an observer. Everywhere I went, I would retreat to one of the corners and look at everything around me, especially people. I don't remember whether I measured the danger they posed to me or the hope that they would be nice to me. I just remember standing silently behind everyone, peeking out and imagining an opportunity to approach me. The truth is that it almost always happened in the opposite way. The most common thing was for them to approach me. The funny thing was that it was always someone who had also been watching me for some time from across the room. Like me. Like two drug addicts who approach and recognise each other by the way they move their bodies and talk. Or two homosexuals. Or two cats under the same light of a lamp. Measuring who is the stronger. Feeling who is the less daring.

All change begins with a provocation. It can't be otherwise. The provocation is life in motion. It is the best of us being called to live. It is not wanting to go through the same thing anymore and to take a different path. Without provocation, everything is mechanical and done without passion. The simplest thing loses by anticipation any sense to happen in a certain time or place. It simply happens, without penance or reward. It just happens, because if it did not happen it would be the same. Just like everything that is not born out of provocation. Or done in a provocative way. It seems lifeless. Mathematical. Illegitimate. Sick. As if even death isn't worth living.

I love you because it is no longer possible for me not to love you. I love you every day with one more letter in my will to write everything I have never written about love. I love you because loving you has made me someone much greater than a simple equation of emotions and feelings. I always feel you differently in the way that each time I welcome and intoxicate you between my hands and lips. Your body listens to me. It feels me. It tells me what no words can tell me. It draws riddles on my skin and tears me with the force of a blow from the sea on the sand. I love you, because one only really loves when love is stronger than any understanding. I love you, because I no longer need the word love to define what I feel. I only need what brings me here. For you. To me.

If you are attracting losses in your life, this is the time to go beyond what you think is coherent and safe, logical and easy. The time has come to stop wanting things that you choose without being for yourself, but rather for what others will think of you. Whenever life does not give you what you would so much like to have, it is because it is not yet the moment or perhaps it never will be. When you want what is not supposed to be yours, you waste time by being where you should no longer be. When you stop wanting whatever it is and start to let yourself go where life wants to take you, without fear, without creating resistance, you will start to experience less loss and less pain. When you begin to leave everything open, you begin to receive the inspiration to feel the true path to follow. It will sound crazy to you. It's going to sound strange to you. But don't worry about anything else. Your light has already been rekindled and your sky is already starting to have stars again.

I feel free when what I do is in harmony with what I feel. I have long understood that my freedom depends only on me. All the excuses I can find for not being so are just excuses to justify my fear of not risking being so. Freedom implies an attitude of respect for who we are, and it is on this point that most of us fail and fall back. Respecting ourselves is not just an obligation. It is above all a choice. When I choose to respect myself in front of those who want to disrespect me, I choose to face my fear of being criticised, judged and not accepted. Being free is also not being afraid of being alone, because solitude is almost always the first step towards freedom. Fear of being alone with ourselves traps us to others. Solitude helps us to feel who we are. Some want to understand. Others run away. To tell the truth, we are the greatest paradox in life. We live little of the much we think we know.

There is another life to live when you let go of fear. There is a different life behind all the fear, a life of tranquillity and calm. Those who have never lived it, never know where they have been. Living without fear is hard, but it is much harder to live in fear. Nothing makes sense. Everything is effort and suffering. Everything is so far from your light. From your original path. From your mission. From everything you never dreamed you could live. Like in a nightmare. Like an unsuccessful escape where fear denounces you at the first step. Merciless. Making you believe that it's not possible to live without remembering it. Whispering that happiness is just a fantasy. A lie. Something you have to forget in order to move on.

Your soul touched mine. Without saying anything. In a way unlike any other. You made yourself felt on my skin. Warm. Intense. Generous. Like a shadow of wind. With a touch like fingers longing only to touch. Without speaking, your soul touched mine. Made me lift my eyes. Made me recognize your gaze. Like in a dream where the eyes insist on not closing. In a flight between lives and magic. In a time tattooed outside of any time. As if you gave me everything before you gave me anything. Not as if it was nothing I expected, but rather everything I never expected to feel.

I have days when I feel like moving cities, leaving alone where nobody knows me, choosing a flat in the middle of many other flats, anonymous, enough to accommodate the few things I would take with me, choosing a cafe lost in a street, sitting down and reading one of the many books I always put off reading. I have days when I feel like changing cities, walking through the crowd whistling songs from my adolescence without shame for my horrible whistling, talking to people I've never seen before, smiling new smiles that I've never smiled in my life, feeling once again the freedom to change places and paths, words and thoughts. I have days when I feel like changing cities, rewriting sentences and tears, leaving with no direction, no destination, no time, without having to look back, to stop accepting what does not belong to me and stay only with what has never been mine yet.

Sometimes, when I least expect it, I feel life inside me with such an intensity that I feel more alive than I ever have before. It's not something I premeditate or want at that moment to feel. It is something that crosses my heart, suddenly, without warning, as if it were an absolute certainty or a still incomprehensible revelation. It almost always happens when I am at my saddest or doubting myself. I too have uncertainties and doubts. I have blood running through my veins and sweat on my skin. Just like in others. Like in those I love or don't know. Or even those who remind me that life is a blessing, especially when I tend for a moment to forget it.

One day, I will have you in front of me. I will finally receive you between my arms and say your name so that you will hear it without any echo or distance. I know that I will recognise your smell, the taste of your kisses, the lightness of your touch, the boldness of your words spoken against my neck, without ever having heard or felt them so close before. I know that I will want very much to take you with me where I have never taken you, even though I know you know where I am taking you. I know you want it as much as I do. No more, no less. The same. Just as I know that you want me as I want you, that you want to tear my skin the way I will heal it later. I know the madness that moves us. The certainty of that which we will no longer need to postpone. Nor sacrifice. Alongside our desires. Of our smiles. Of our sky finally marked by the total inexistence of time.

I try to understand those who seem to wait for something they don't even know what it is. Something about them reminds me of the moment when I leave from where I never wanted to be. Their immobility has the same texture as an endless tumble. I guess, but don't see, a despair of death before death in their inexpressive faces, faces that no portrait can bear. I try to understand them, but I can't. There is something in their waiting that anguishes me, as if they were waiting in silence for a poison without antidote to carry them to where they already are without knowing they already are. I can't understand those who rip the life out of the heart and let it beat without urgency or hope. I believe there is always a path not yet travelled. A poem yet to be written. A love to live. A time within another time. A little more of me beyond who I have ceased to be.

Each morning I give thanks. Not for what I want, but for what is already with me. I have long since learned that I don't need anything more than what I have to take the next step in my life. Everything else is just excuses I can make up so I don't have to deal with the possibility of failure or my lack of courage to be happy. Many people talk about wanting to be happy, but at the same time they tolerate too much misfortune in their lives to ever come close to happiness. It sounds like a contradiction or a big lie, but the truth is that many people are afraid of happiness, only because they do not know or dream what it is like to be happy. What they don't know makes them hesitate and retreat. The fear of suffering with the chance of not achieving happiness is greater than the fear of feeling it. Only those who are not afraid of losing anything are happy. The others only talk about what they do not know.

If you are depressed, you can be sure that you are not weak. You just tried for too long to be who you no longer wanted to be, you endured suffering beyond what you thought you were capable of, you pushed yourself above what you should have and knew, just to have peace. That was all. Now it is your turn to give yourself time, to respect yourself, to stop missing yourself.

I am no longer afraid to remember you. You no longer hurt me. I already know how to live without your image. I've died too many times wanting to live for you. Nothing that I suffered in your presence and in your absence is bad anymore. I learned to see what it is without you. I learned to see myself without tears and silences. I began to build myself up knowing that you would not destroy me next. I gained a gentle urgency to be with me. A mute joy that sounds like songs of arrival. A desire to embrace me as you have never been able to do. Without too much possession, nor too little lassitude. As if that's all I needed to live again. In a glimpse of life. In a happiness already without you. Only with me. As I've never known.

When you choose to survive rather than live, you are putting aside your greatest purpose in life, which is to be happy. If you stop having a purpose, nothing that happens has anything to do with you anymore, but only with your suffering and pain. Your purpose is what allows you to feel the participation of your spirit in the construction of who you are and of everything that makes you smile with joy. Without purpose, nothing spiritual happens in your life. You may even be religious, but if you survive, you become dependent on things that have nothing to do with your purpose. You deceive yourself with the idea that life is difficult, that you have to be very lucky and struggle a lot. If you look fearlessly into your heart, you will understand that none of this is true or makes any sense. You will finally understand that to survive is really not to have confidence in yourself. It means not believing in heaven. It means losing all faith in what you do not yet see. It means not wanting answers to the questions that you stopped asking long ago. Just like that. As are all the strangest ways of being in life.

What you think about, creates the same in your life. Thoughts of a certain nature create an identical nature for you. The impact of these phrases frightens those who cannot stop systematically thinking about things they do not want in their lives. The fear of living them makes you actually live them. For some time, I myself was frightened by this idea and tried to change my thoughts. I came to the conclusion that it is impossible to have this capacity without a great deal of effort and dedication which, at the same time, prevents me from experiencing emotions such as sadness and pain, which are so important for me to rediscover my joy. My path made me realise that what I do is more important than what I think. So I began to counteract the less good of what I think with the opposite attitude. Whenever I think of the fear of being unhealthy, I will do something good for my body. Whenever my thoughts are of fear for something, I do something that shows that I'm thinking the opposite way. In fact, what I am doing is creating an energy that is stronger than that of my thoughts, that is, the energy of my actions. Today, I know that the important thing is no longer what I think, but the actions I take to counteract the less good essence of those same thoughts. So simple. Like everything else that really matters in my life.

To be someone, you don't need to do anything. You are already someone. The question is whether you want that someone enough for them to become who you truly are. When you wait for someone to tell you, you will always be someone that others allow you to be. It is only when you don't need anyone to tell you that you begin to create who you have always been without daring to be. The truth is that the more you are, the less people demand that you do something to show who you are. From the moment you are yourself, they accept you or reject you. There is no middle ground. The truth is that there are many people who have a strange need to worship or destroy what they love and need so much. That's all and nothing more.

Every dream has its path. It always ends in a smile. If it doesn't, it becomes a cage without doors or sun. A space of memories that we want to come alive once more, but which is too close to its death to be able to open its eyes and walk again. To dream is not only to go after dreams. Dreaming is above all not chasing dreams, but rather having them on our side every day. Nothing can be more tangible than a dream, otherwise it is just something intangible and almost haunting. Every dream has to have a smell all of its own, a unique texture. It has to be an extension of the dreamer, a guarantee of life beyond any pain or suffering. That is why dreaming is only for some. It is for those for whom dreams never take away from the present moment.

Sometimes in the place of life seems to be an absence. I don't know how to explain it or even justify it. I just feel it as a presence without a name, without a story. It stays there, quiet, with me, without manifesting itself, but also without leaving. It seems to want only to keep me at arm's length with its silence so that I cannot free myself from what I feel. I don't even know if what I feel is mine. I only know that I feel an absence in his presence. Almost an emptiness without being. A kind of shadow without sun. A time without anything that allows me to recognise myself. Sometimes I close my eyes and cover my ears, but it's no use to me. It remains there without being. It stays without letting me know where it came from. I want to believe that it doesn't want to harm me because as it appears, it disappears and I feel like smiling again. I don't know what it is, but I know that one day it will reveal itself to me. If I don't show fear. If I don't send it away.

It's not our time yet. We both know it. It's not enough to love each other. Life must allow us to celebrate our love together. There is a proper time for each thing and everything. Just as there have been other times in our history at more distant and less obvious times.

We have felt our way once more, but we are still wanderers. We don't know if the distance between us is a perpetual sentence or a truce between lives. We know only that which unites us. A love that memory cannot erase. The desire to one day finally touch each other's hand. Something as simple as that. But only ours.

I can't understand those who pretend to forget just so as not to suffer. Sometimes there are people who have the ambition of wanting to cheat time, when nothing is more consistent and biting than time itself. There are people who think they forget, just because they don't remember. They are not aware that the mind has the capacity to hide what seems to be out of sight. One day, for a reason unique to life, they realise that it was always there, that it never left its corner waiting for the moment when oblivion would fall away. Sometimes it is too late to understand that running away from something is always bringing it closer. There is no point in wanting to forget what still remains alive. There is always a moment when it reappears. Like the north wind by the beach. Like a stamp on the back of an undated letter. Just so that you suffer a little more and can finally see a new way out. Maybe with a new pain. But also with a new life.

I have never been a good student of Portuguese. In the years following the twenty-fifth of April, when one could pass with a failing grade in three or four subjects, Portuguese, together with mathematics, was immediately nominated to be ignored. I remember the difficulty I had applying verbs in their correct tenses and interpreting any texts that the teachers presented in class. I had no idea what the direct and indirect complement were and when they applied before or after the verb. I prayed every day not to be called to the blackboard or to enter a class devoted to composition. I had a terrible lack of imagination. Even when the topic was free, I couldn't choose one. I couldn't find a way to write more than six or seven lines, and often my text was chosen and read in the next class as the worst of all. I smiled together with my classmates while the teacher read it out loud, but the feeling that went through my chest was to tell everyone and everything to go fuck themselves. I began to hate the Portuguese language and its authors. Eça, Garrett, Gil, Pessoa, and the execrable Camões. I couldn't like a single stanza of Os Lusíadas and I think I deliberately lost the book at least three times in the same year. The truth is that I graduated without any love for my language and its grammatical constructions. When I started to feel like writing, I marvelled at the fluid way I did it. Even today, I write much more easily than I understand Portuguese. The truth is that I write in a language that I still neither understand nor want to understand. I don't want to do anything else for it either. I am like this and I will continue to be this way. A writer without rules. Without influences. Without the need to please anyone. Free and without contraindications. Like a missing medicine for a disease with no cure.

My sleep is not always peaceful. There are times when I wake up for no reason, as if someone whispered in my ear that it is better to be awake at that moment. I look with my eyes open towards the dark and I stay alert, not for fear of anything, but just to be able to feel the silence of the night over my thoughts. The truth is that I often welcome the arrival of the dawn without sleep. I wake up slowly while more than half the world is still asleep. I don't rebel or try to go back to sleep. I open the shutter and let the light flood my room. I lie back down and smile. I accept that something in life has a yearning to find me early. I sit up in bed and pray with myself. I am grateful for what I am yet to experience, because I always like to be grateful for what I don't know. They say that gratitude manifests itself when we can feel life. I believe more that it is when we are able to accept what life makes us feel. Like when we love without knowing we are loving. Like a dancer who falls and smiles because he knows that ease is the enemy of what one wants to be great.

I never wanted to change my past. Not even when I suffered or died of fear. I think I understood very early on that there was no point in me renouncing it or wanting it any other way. It had been the way it had been and I accepted it the way I chose to live it. The responsibility for its outcome is mine and nobody else's. I was the one who lived it and not anyone else. That's fair enough. If it hadn't turned out the way it did, I myself would be different from who I am. And that, I don't want. I love my carefree and generous way of living with myself. I am no god or hero full of decorations. I am someone who has earned his place under this dance of sun and moon. Of love and madness. Of vices and desires. A place I give only to the one I know I will always love.

My best talent always manifests itself when I do what seems obvious once done. It is something that has always existed within me. Like a birthmark hidden by layers of skin and many other signs. It's what sets me apart from other people. It doesn't make me better. Nor worse. Rather it makes me live away from the normality I abhor. Like my favourite dream, made of the unforeseen and unexpected. With no one else but me. The dreamer with talent. The man who dreams with his eyes open. With an addiction to life. With a huge will to erase destinies and choose always new paths.

I can't live without the idea of always wanting to change my world. I've never liked things that are static, still, lifeless. I need to know the movement and angles of everything around me. I am a kind of fish that dares to want to climb trees, even at the imminent risk of losing half my scales on the way up. I am not stubborn, but I am determined. When I want something, I do everything I feel is within my power and let life do the rest. I've always known that life conspires in my favour if I do the same. It's a never-ending celebration. A moment forever. Like when I choose with my heart and silence fear. I gag it without mercy. No more fear of fear. No more fear of what is to come and stay. Just because I have the ability to be who I want to be. Always. On a path very much my own. Mine alone. Like my smile when I wake up. Every morning.

Accept it. Accept what you are experiencing at this moment. Do not try to change without first accepting, because you will not achieve anything new. Acceptance is the basis of change and the key to all commitment. Especially with yourself. A commitment that frees you and does not imprison you. A commitment in which you are doing what you should do for yourself. Nothing more. Heaven thanks you and you evolve. The others do not understand and you can help. If they want you to. If they are prepared. If they do not think they are more or better than you. Out of sheer survival. For stupidity. Like meaningless words spoken in a time that escapes everyone without mercy.

My life was never about luck, but rather about choices. It was never something I waited for, but something I felt happening with every decision. For a long time now I have not chosen what interests me, but only what I love. Everything around me has to be about me, otherwise it no longer stays on my side. I may even sound like an idealist to some, but the truth is that life is mine and I make of it what I want. I decided a good few years ago to no longer condone lies or arrogance, lack of humility or hypocrisy, and to commit myself to always remaining free. Freedom is my greatest commitment to myself. I do not allow anyone to pinch or threaten me, because I know that without freedom, I die. I don't even exist. Nor do I feel. I die. Only because I remember the time when I was free and flew above the clouds, where one day I forgot that if I stopped feeling the wind I could be trapped again.

Not all people understand my way of being a Coach. I understand them. Everything that is not normal or formatted is scary. It becomes a risk. It can turn out to be a failure. A lost time with someone who only knows how to move when provoked. The truth is that I believe that where there is no provocation, there is normality and predictability, more of the same and everything that does not make you go further. I fully understand what I provoke, but I don't know how to be any other way. Whoever risks seeking me out knows what I am talking about. I don't use disguises and I don't pressure. I don't waste time with those who stall and deceive. I am clear in what I say and ask. I challenge only to the extent of who I have in front of me. I don't try to sound like what I'm not, or what I want people to think about me. I am sensitive to the point of putting myself in the shoes of those who come to me and reading their silence. It's not a talent. It's a passion. It's wanting very much to get the hell out of every heart.

To have faith is to value the unthinkable in the face of the imperfect. It is allowing yourself to have a space of your own to grow in respect and dignity for yourself. My faith is made in equal parts of silence and smiles. It is a side of me that has become as natural as the other. I have above all faith in myself. I have learned to trust who I have become and to not attach anything to the end result of anything. I started to feel faith as my very own way of meditating and evolving. My evolution has nothing to do with what I believe, but with how I live my life. I no longer deny anything of what I feel. Nor what I live. My faith in myself does not allow it. Quite the contrary. It helps me to approach life with the feeling that everything is possible for me as long as I never forget that I am no better than anyone else. Nor worse. Just me. Without any fear of being so.

Almost nobody knows me. Some people assume they know who I am, but the truth is that I am not the easy type to be understood. Rarely do my answers have anything to do with the questions I am asked. Rather, it has to do with how I feel about the people who ask me. I believe I speak a language of life, but many think I'm capable of what I don't need to be capable of. Those who don't know me don't know the simplicity of my spirit. Things are for me what they are, without illusions or lies, and perhaps for that reason they see in me what I am not even remotely being, in this mania to complicate what is simple. Those who can feel what I write beyond what I write, are the closest to know me only for what I am. My truth is not always in what I write, but in what remains unwritten between each word. What I keep only for myself. What I don't like to share with anyone, not for fear of exposing myself, but just because I like to keep secrets about myself. So simple. Just like that. As my heart and soul always are.

Life calls me every day. It wants me to get out of all kinds of doldrums and live each of the adventures it proposes. It asks me to be myself in everything I choose and live. It tells me that I know better than anyone what smells like me and is supposed to be on my side. It makes me believe that everything else does not matter, because everything else always happens naturally and freely. Life asks me to feel its love until I feel nothing else on my skin. Like a perfume. A mark. A code for a freedom that not even birds know. A freedom made only by me.

My inspiration is always in who I am. Life has given me the ability to be able to write about everything I feel. I know I am part of a whole, but I also know I am unique. I never compare myself to anyone so as not to fall into the temptation of demanding something of myself or diminishing myself. I am not like anyone and no one is like me.

Everyone's difference is where their true talent lies. Talents happen when you discover your most passionate side. Passion exists only when you are who you are. So simple, yet so inaccessible. Like the antidote without a poison. Like longing without a heart.

Everything I feel in me is to make me be myself. It's no use for me to feel and do nothing. I have understood that not following what I feel is the same as not wanting what came to stay with me. I already know that everything I intuit I do, even if I will never know the reason why I am doing it. I accept that I have within me a wisdom that only wants my well-being. I don't always understand it, but I never question it. Some things are so simple that they also seem so strange. But the truth is that they are surprising. They bring life. They have a will of their own. They are part of who I am.

I no longer naively believe in people. I have long since stopped giving importance to those who talk too much about themselves or always have an easy solution for the lives of others. Words always carry the soul of the person who says them. It can't be otherwise. Who speaks without soul, lies or does not believe in what he speaks. The truth is that he who speaks without soul, not even his silence deceives me anymore. But to speak with soul is not only to speak with enthusiasm. To speak with soul is to understand the reason for one's mistakes. It means knowing that whoever is listening also has a soul. It means feeling the movement of your own wings on your back.

A long time ago I stopped wanting the immediate and the comfortable. A long time ago I stopped wanting only to survive. A long time ago I no longer want to feel good just to escape from suffering. I've known for a long time that I have an inexperienced soul, but one that already speaks to me without intermediaries or manipulations, that touches me more and more in my heart as a child without sense. It is it that tells me not to run away from pain, from emotions, from confrontation, from the unknown, from sensitivity. It is it that whispers to me truths that make me smile so heartfelt, truths that I welcome and feel as parts of myself. The truth is that I no longer run away from anything it makes me feel. I know that it is me in my purest state, in that sacred state that fears nothing and nobody, in that light that wants to make me fly above all limits and demands.

I like my life not to have a lot of repetition. I'd much rather change the way I do many of my things than allow myself to do them in effort or by excess. I love changing the way I do everything, most of all because sameness unsettles me, takes away the fun, takes me away from my journey. The truth is I wasn't born to repeat. Rather, I was born to create everything that keeps me away from repetition.

I am nothing of what many people think about me. I am a rebel, it is true, but I also know how to be gentle and generous with those who love life as much as I do. I am bold, indeed, but I am also thoughtful enough to know how to distinguish truth from lies, even in those who say nothing to me or lower their gaze. I am courageous, without doubt, even without sword or shield, without palace or castle, without coat of arms or title. I am courageous only because I am not afraid to leave behind what is not supposed to be with me anymore and I do not allow myself to give up what has my light. I am a dreamer, an eternal dreamer, because for me dreaming is above all a way of relating to myself. I am a madman, very mad, really very mad, but not to the point of letting my madness be exempt from love and passion and capable of killing myself without smiling. Deep down, it is always me, only me, no matter what I do, because I don't want to be anyone else but myself, a stranger unafraid to meet myself, a demon excommunicated from hell for having a soul and a heart of an angel. Always and only.

It's interesting to realise that there are people waiting to know my weaknesses and my most perfidious secrets to denounce me in the public square. From what I've seen throughout my life, that's how it works with everyone who stands out for being different. You don't have to be better. It is enough to be different. The possibility of them accepting that what irritates them about me is nothing more than what they need to work on in them is remote, because those who criticize and judge don't hypothesize that they are wrong. Accepting that would be worse than being able to read their thoughts. Basically, agreeing with such a truth would work like admitting that they think and feel inferior in the relationship they have with those they insist on criticizing and judging. No one who criticises allow themselves to be helped. No one who judges wants to be found out. The truth is that even if one day my weaknesses and my most perfidious secrets are exposed in the public square, I have not said or promised anyone that I would be perfect, nor that I would stop living everything I want to live. This is who I am. A man unafraid of being imperfect and full of the will to be daring.

A lot of new things are happening in my life. Sometimes I find myself smiling incredulously but understanding the reason why everything is happening. It may seem somehow presumptuous or even selfish, but everything has improved since the moment I realised I was good. However, good is not about being better than someone or everyone. I am good because what I choose and do is first and foremost good for me. Good, when it comes from the soul, attracts more good. It has no secret. I am good because I allowed myself to take risks, to fail as many times as necessary until I discovered my talents. When I discovered them, I never stopped knowing them and recognizing myself in them. The truth is that we all have talents. There is no point in remaining indifferent to this truth. Those who do not risk seeking theirs, become just a ghost haunted by themselves. A shadow without sun. A cry without an echo. An invisible among the blind. Nothing more than this.

When I see you, I am completely driven mad by the desire to make you mine. The way you smile and move your shoulders works like a punch in my stomach. I find it hard to stay calm when you approach and say my name. I feel my heart beating at the speed of a chase. My will clenches my veins, prevents the blood from flowing free. It turns me into a controlled animal, a beast innocent of its ferocity. I imagine with you what I can't imagine with anyone else. You have the talent to bring out my most brutal side, the one I have always kept secret from myself. With you, I feel like a formless demon. An angel adrift. An assassin capable of killing for desire. And for love.

Sometimes I need to disconnect from everything, to fly to that place of my own and no one else's where no one else gets in but me. Not even the one I love. Disconnecting is for me an act that only makes sense if done alone. When I switch off, I approach that point where nothing affects me more than what I allow. There, I learn to make myself fragile and not to fear my own fragility. I have long understood that when I become fragile I stop resisting what I feel. I stop wanting to control anything. I allow myself to feel everything, especially love, without wanting to run away from it any more, without turning my heart's face to its more invisible side. I let love hurt me while it hurts me, because I also know that the truth of love is in the essence of the pain it causes me. I welcome the pain. I accept it and let it grow until it no longer hurts, until it makes me feel the love behind it. All pain is made of love. All love is born from a pain inside me. Like this. Just like this.

When the time comes to receive, I'm not afraid of not deserving. Life is not made only of suffering. It is also made of graces. Receiving is a grace that life grants me when I learn the lesson and change my attitude. The truth is that I receive from life in proportion to the respect I show for myself. That is why, when I receive, I smile and toast, because I know that I deserve every single thing that comes my way. Just as I deserve the smile that someone up there is toasting me with. Of this I am sure.

Everything that life doesn't put on my side, it's because it's not supposed to be with me. At least, not now. Maybe later. I don't know, and I don't want to know. Life is this moment and no other. It is gratitude for being alive and experiencing what I feel. It is an energy at my disposal. It is an endless adventure. If it has an end it is no longer an adventure. It's just a memory. And I don't want to have time to remember. I want to have time only to live. Because the truth is I don't want to change life. I just want to fly my own way in its company.

I have long since decided to go my own way. I allow less than the fingers of a handful of people to be part of it. Don't get me wrong. I respect everyone, but I allow few to be close to me. I am not arrogant or elitist, but I have known for a long time that no one knows how to have more than a handful of friends. I know a lot of people I like. I know many more who come in and out of my life with the validity and speed of a vaccine. I always learn something from each of them, but they are not always lessons in respect or freedom. It is from them that I understand that teachings can be cruel and painful. But that's OK. Learning is also having a sense of humour. It's knowing how to smile at those who want to take our smiles away.

The sea is like a hand gesture. A bolder touch on the texture of all the places of my body. Even the ones I ignore or don't know. The most delicate ones or the ones that bring me proof of the existence of life in me. Like waves. Tides. Storms. Like stories and lost parts that merge together when I enter it and decide never to leave. That sea is yours too, it reminds me of you, it alchemises my whole heart in equal layers of love and desire, of sun and salt, of words and silences. That sea is all that I am on your skin.

My silence is who I am when I stay with myself. The habit of noise is stronger than the need to break it. We live too fast, but almost always without a defined start or a goal with a name of its own. Silence is that place where you stop running without wanting to get anywhere. You are in it and you stay. That's all. Just like me. I have learned to feel myself in my silence, to know myself there, to become attached to its sound and to everything that naturally brings me to mind. I'm not interested in not thinking. I prefer to let my silence take me where it always wanted me to go. I like it better that it directs me. Only it can give me a journey without having to give me a destination.

There are people who will never understand freedom when it interferes in their lives. They talk about freedom, but silently fear it more than they fear themselves. The truth is that living with someone free and not wanting to imprison them is one of the greatest talents anyone can demonstrate. It is not for everyone. In fact, it is for very few. Freedom has that bit of irony that brings out the lie in those who insist on hiding it. There are no known antidotes. Nor is there an immediate cure. Freedom always bothers those who do not know how to liberate.

I like women who give me what I never thought I wanted. I like women who tease and surprise me as if nothing was premeditated. I like women who hide under a smile a thousand other smiles. I like women who are wildly docile and savages. I like women who also know how to make love like men. I like women who shatter calendars and break compasses. I like women who fall in love with me without ceasing to fall even more in love with themselves. I like women who tear my mouth open with a kiss so that they can drink my blood. I like women who know how to be women.

When life wants two people to learn at the same time, it connects them. The lesson may not be the same, but the action links them together. One may one day suffer from the liberation of the other and the second may learn from the loss of the first. They may even learn the same thing. The important thing is not so much whether they learn or not, but whether they will want to live what life is proposing to them. Many run away because they no longer want or believe in another life. Many others remain quiet, as if they could pass unscathed and unnoticed through life. Only very few accept to live what frightens them, only because they no longer have any doubts that behind every fear there is always a new word of unwritten love.

Love is worthless without fear. I have long known that every feeling is strengthened in the presence of its opposite. All of the same is the same as nothing. Only that which replaces something that hurts is valued. Love always grows in opposition to fear. To live in one is to not live in the other. Both exist, but only one prevails in my heart. Love. Only it. Only it. Because I deserve it.

Today, I believe that all pain eventually passes. Its timing depends on my decision to accept it. When I am grateful, I accept it. When I accept it, I can finally understand it and transform it. No pain is everlasting. It lasts only as long as I allow it to have power over me. Life is always generous. If it hurts it is because it also brings a cure. The cure is always in my attitude. Only and in no other side of me.

I always let go of people who are too attached to me. I want free people with me, people who know how to live with themselves too. Dependency is the anti-life. It is the fear of losing. It is the rejection of oneself. In my life I need people who are happy, uncomplicated, confident, not afraid of feeling afraid. I cannot have patience for people who prefer to live with the idea that the world has turned its back on them, with the conviction that they are worth nothing or very little. I have always been bothered by condescension in exaggeration and the need for approval. I like someone who understands what they're doing here, who dares to go forward unarmed, who trust themselves more than anyone else, who knows that without freedom nothing significant happens in life. I like those who like themselves more than me.

Love life. Only that, without expecting anything. Love it for what it is, without wanting it to be different. Love it as it is, without asking for anything more or wanting anything in return. Love it completely, without fear of losing it, without fearing it or wanting to change it. Love it for all that it teaches you about yourself. Love it more than you have ever loved anyone. Love it and feel your love for it grow every day. Love it, because the true charm of life is in all the love you feel for it. Here and now.

I am no longer afraid to believe in what I feel. The truth is that in this way I open myself to what I cannot know in any other way. If I don't run away from what I feel, I feel even more and I get closer and closer to loving what I feel. I don't need to understand anything at all, but only to believe and smile. The most serene path always comes when I follow what I feel. True life reveals itself when I listen to myself above everything and everyone. I may even feel afraid, but I know that I have become brave and delicate from the moment I stopped having doubts about what my heart tells me. These are not secrets, nor are they revelations, they are requests. It asks me to stop worrying, to choose only what makes my eyes smile, to never give up believing in love. It asks me above all not to want to understand anything, because only what I feel is true. Nothing more.

Don't let anything disturb you. Do not allow anything to take away your peace. Do not allow anyone to enter your life who does not understand or like you. Free your spirit from everything that ties you to a place where you no longer want to stay. Go to those places that call to your soul. Quiet your mind and open your heart. Do not think about anything that will make you think even more. Just feel, as if feeling is pulling something towards you until it touches you. And stay. Just stay and feel your skin and your heart. Feel what you feel and let it be. Just do it. That is how you always start on a new path. Even if you don't know anything yet. It does not matter.

I never want to explain how I feel about you. I always lose. I'd rather just smile when remembering you. It's my way of saying I think of you. If you could look at me now, you would see a man with a silly smile on his lips, his hands playing with his curly hair, his eyes fixed on the sky, way up there where not even the gods reach. Even though you're not here, I feel you close to me, glued to my body, in an embrace that engraves silences on my skin. I always find it difficult to explain in words what you have tattooed on my heart. I prefer to look at you and smile. I know you read me. Everything I am with you was written by you.

There is something pacifying in the rain when it falls hard on dry land. The smell it releases reminds us of the beginning of things, that instant when everything is born in the innocence of not knowing that one day it will also die. The sound carries us like the current of a river to the sea, makes us close our eyes and smile, in silence, like in a free and godless prayer. I have known rain since I can remember standing at the windows and watching it crash noisily on the panes. It has always attracted me. I am not sure how to explain it, but I believe it has to do with my origins. I was born on a very rainy December day, eyes open from the first second, face slightly twisted from the suction cups and irons used to save me from dying of asphyxiation at birth, and I must have heard the sound of the rains on the windows and the roof of the maternity hospital as a harbinger of life, there where I smiled for the first time still not knowing that one day I too will die.

The most frivolous part of my soul is my body, because it is the one that makes me feel indecency in a unique and divine way. Innocence bores me. Shyness sometimes seduces me. Neediness makes me by instinct manipulative. Sex, that one, drives me mad, if it's done right. It has to kill me before it even starts. It has to rip out my chest before it even makes me close my eyes. It has to be dangerous, capable of taking me where I never thought I'd go. It has to penetrate my skin before my body. It has to be at the same time carnal and spiritual, mad and generous, like a love that never dies or does not know that it is eternal. It has to take my clothes off without ever letting me feel clothed. It has to be storm. Only storm

.

There are days when you are in my heart. You touch me with the lightness of a kiss and leave me almost flat. When you persist in staying inside it, nothing else remains the same in me. I smile without ever having stopped smiling, I close my eyes without even opening them once, I place my hands on my chest so that I can feel in each palm the warmth of your presence and realise that you are still there. There are days when you grab my heart and don't let go until you decide to fall asleep. Then I watch you sleep as if I was watching the birth of a different horizon, of a new sun that leaves no shadows, of a sea with the same taste as endless love. There are days when you mark my heart, not with scars or even wounds, but only with a trail of stars that leads me indefinitely to you. When I finally reach you, I feel a heaven enter inside me. Not just any sky. It's a sky unlike any other. It's a sky made inside my sky. I don't even need to see it to know it's a sky with your name on it. No less than that. No more than that. Just with your name.

Disrespect attracts disrespect. Allowing myself to stay in a job where I am disrespected is the same as disrespecting myself every day. To stay in a relationship where I feel disrespected is to be disrespecting myself each and every moment. The person I have become is the image of all the disrespect I admit in my life. Disrespect attracts only disrespect. If I want to change all this, I must start respecting myself in all my choices. The mission to regain my respect is an attitude. Every change of attitude is a new path to walk. It is above all amplifying the love I give myself, doing to myself only what I would like others to do to me. That is all. Nothing else.

I don't run away from what seems impossible. Life has shown me many times that I can be wrong about what I think. I need to be an archaeologist of myself and find within who I am who I want to be. Discovering who I want to be allows me to understand that the impossible only exists in my disbelief about the possible. If I think I am incapable of something, the possibility of going further is soon put aside. I die before I even lose air. Nothing is worthwhile if it does not put me in question. I like the impossible because I risk being defeated. I risk understanding that winning is of no use, not even to keep everything. I have known for a long time that everything is at the same time nothing and little of almost nothing. Like the impossible that I always insist on making possible. Close to me. Between ideas of a new world and armies of much love.

I'm in love with a mermaid. The sea brought us together as in a song. It made of us a path of stars. A trail of seashells. A handful of blessed salt. The sea brought us together and smiled. It did with us what heaven asked of it. It united us in a bond of wind. It christened our love with its name. It called it sea. It didn't want it to have another. It could have no other. A name as long as a kiss. Only one. The most unique. Ours. A kiss made only of waves and tides. A kiss with memory. Without end. Only without end.

I believe that we go through everything we go through to one day know how to love. The pain and all the suffering, the joys and the laughter, the sadness and the frustration, the opportunities and the failures, the resistance and the tiredness, everything happens so that we can recognize love in them. If we don't recognise it, we won't be able to feel it or learn it. We will not know how to seek the best in ourselves. We will never know how to love. We will only want to anticipate what in truth has long since left us behind. There is too much time to be worthwhile. Stories without history. Stories without love.

I've been wanting to understand love. I don't want to see it as something that has to go right, because right isn't always the best thing for anyone. I don't like to think of it as a mistake, because I've made a lot of mistakes and I've learnt a lot more from my mistakes than from my cowardice. I can't associate it with any kind of patience, because patience is something I already have little of and I don't intend to force myself to feel it. I also don't want to think of it as an attempt, because those who try are always very likely to fail or give up halfway through. I'm just trying to understand love. That's all.

There is hell in many hearts. Sadness has long ceased to be sadness and has turned into anguish. There is poison running inside the veins of many and muffled screams against the skin of arms. Sleep slips away with each passing hour of the night. Eyes dry up in the silence of already weeping without tears. It's no use wanting to smile if the smile died in the need to get ahead of the world. Rigidity killed it with the coldness of a serial killer. It took its life for being different. It didn't want it alive for disturbing normality. The truth is that few people allow joy anymore because they can't bear to see it in others. They prefer to forget that they ever wanted to be happy. They prefer to kill angels so that they can bury their wings. Drown mermaids so that their song cannot be heard. All in the name of what no longer even deserves a name. Everything so that someone doesn't take the little they still have.

If you feel guilt, get drunk on life. You are the one who attracts everything, so celebrate. Everything that happens to you is caused by who you are being. If you don't like what you experience, change your attitude. Fuck those who fuck you. Fuck those who don't respect you. Fuck those who say bad things about you for no reason. Choose to be free, even if it means losing everything. You can be sure that on that day, even with nothing, you will be much happier.

I like to let myself be between my sky and my house. I have the habit of sitting on my balcony and closing my eyes. I hear what nobody else hears, because what I hear has no sound. I listen to memories and smiles. I hear voices and review faces. I hear places and smells. I travel in the middle of times and distances and I give myself back the unrepeatable. When I return, I no longer want to go back. I brought everything I needed to bring.

There are people who want to make life a mathematical problem. Two plus two must always equal four. Others like to turn it into an inaccessible magic formula that only a few enlightened people can access. Others believe that life is only suffering and pain, sacrifices and death, greed and complaints, unhappiness and tears. I, for my part, have long seen life as a gift. I live each instant. That is all. I live. Because living is letting life call me. From the inside out. Like a shell. From the pearl to the ocean.

It is interesting the relationship men have with me. With a few exceptions, they love me without knowing or understanding it. They don't tell me because it would be strange even for them. They love me because love is often hidden behind the greatest contempt. They love me because they can't hate me and they rebel because they don't feel able to tell me. The truth is that they do not understand that the love they feel for me is a reflection of the love they need to feel for themselves. They do not understand that the fear they feel for my presence is a reflection of the fear they feel for not feeling able to stand up and live their own life. They secretly want to be who I am because they don't understand that they can be so much more to themselves. They can be everything they dream of being. They can be endless love. A smile. A life that is beautiful to die for. Theirs and theirs alone.

I feel myself being reborn to a new life. I feel it like a caress that I am not yet allowed to see. I only feel it. Nothing more. I know it already exists, because I have it, but I cannot see it yet. It is a new life that vibrates louder, more intensely, more freely. It is a new life with the colour of more life. It is a rebirth. It is my time to become unmistakable. Not better, because I don't want to stand out. Not worse, because I don't want to be disrespected. Just unique. Just myself. More authentic. More passionate. With more life in me. In a leap with no net and no fear.

I cannot only see what I want to see. I also need to see what I stubbornly say I don't see. If I don't, I won't actually be able to see anything at all. I will be nothing more than a blind man in a world of illusionists. Reality will always scare me, because I believe every time it is made of pain and lies. I need to dare to see what really exists, what I run away from, what I fear to love, to look at the depth of my sky, the night and the stars, your eyes. If I continue not to see, I will die without stopping breathing. I'll hide with my feet out. I'll be what I wasn't meant to be. If I continue not to see, I will gouge my eyes out without feeling any pain. I'll laugh and cry without understanding what the point of doing so is. I'll be yours before I'm even mine. If I persist in not wanting to see, I will miss the spectacle of the salvation of my soul, even before I leave in the direction of a heaven that I will not be able to recognise, not even with my eyes open.

Today, I found myself dancing alone and smiling like a kid without a clock or a time to come back. I loved feeling the free movement of my body and the ticking of my feet on the floor. I kept a rhythm that sounded natural. I admired myself. I've always been more of a listener than a dancer. I think age has loosened me up, made me bolder. Today, I am able to surpass myself where before I diminished myself. My attitude has changed because I stopped listening so much to others and started to decide more for myself. It may even sound selfish, but it's actually inspiration. A victory over mediocrity and my past.

I like to feel life in my skin. I am very much skin. I need the touch, the contact, the taste. I can't get enough of the smell, the sound and the closeness. I'm addicted to touch. I need to touch, because when I touch, I feel much beyond what I touch. I feel things I have never felt before, things that go through my body, that paint my heart with colours I have never seen, that fill my soul with sweets and dreams. I am of touch, because I don't know how to be any other way. I like to look, but if I don't touch, I seem not to see. I like to smell, but if I don't touch the perfume, I can't close my eyes and smile. I like to listen, but if I don't touch the sound, I don't feel the essence of what I hear. The truth is that the things I have felt most in life, I had to touch. I needed to feel their texture and warmth, their contours and movements. I am no stranger to my appetite for touch. It comes naturally to me. I was born with it. It is part of my seduction to the world.

I have been happy since I stopped controlling. I chose to open myself to life without thinking about whether it would hurt a lot or almost nothing, whether I would love doing it or not. I stopped wanting to anticipate others and myself, feelings and above all emotions. I let it hurt without running away from the pain. I let it make me smile without finding it strange how long each smile lasts. I stopped being afraid of people. I stopped wanting anything more from anything and accepted everything that was with me. I let go of what had to go. I allowed everything to stay that was meant to stay. And I accepted to receive what my life wanted to give me. Every single day. Without fear. Because accepting to receive is the same as living without fear of losing.

Like yourself enough to get out of where you are not respected, be it a job, a relationship or a place. Deal with the fear of losing what hasn't been yours for a long time. Leave before they push you out. Choose before they take away your ability to smile. You are someone special. Behave like one.

I have the sensitivity and acuity of an angel who has forgotten to be an angel. I feel what almost nobody can feel. I see what few can see. I am no better or worse than anyone else. I am only different from everyone and I accept my difference like few others. I refuse to compare myself with anyone. I avoid thinking like others. I push away everything and everyone who wants to change me against my will. Everything in my life is simple. If it is not, I make it so. I do not want more. I do not accept less. Just like that. Simply.

Many of us promise things we know we will never deliver. We do so only to excuse ourselves for our inability to carry them out. When we promise to do something, we momentarily free ourselves from the responsibility of not yet doing it. Normally, we attach a deadline to each promise, because otherwise we wouldn't need to promise anything and we would have already done it. Promising is almost always putting it off forever. A meaningless story. A shot in the foot. An ease allowed by our cleverness as chronic losers. Those who do, don't promise. They never promise. They surprise.

I don't dream to make my life bearable. That would be madness. My dreams exist so that they can make my life even better. I do not deceive myself. I do not mislead myself. But I don't know how to breathe if I can't dream. I do not know how to write without dreaming. I don't know how to live if I cannot dream. My life is a dream because in truth I have never given up dreaming. Not even when I almost let my dreams be killed. There was one that always survived. Mine. The one that nobody knows. The one that makes me know the right time for each thing. The one that opens my heart to let out all the love. A dream without sorrow. Without judgment. The dream of someone who has learned to shine by her own light. That is all.

The people who come into my life are the ones my soul most desires, even though it may seem otherwise. They are almost always the people I least want to see and who torment me the most. They are the ones who don't come to tell me if there is life after death or to question the eternity I believe in. They are the ones who come to show me where they believe I am wrong, where they believe I have done nothing to understand that many things have long since stopped making any sense in my life. My soul claps its hands in front of my stupidity. It calls me every possible name and stubbornly insists that I be reborn from a part of my life that I seem to have forgotten. The challenge is tough because I have to forget the other part, the one where I cling to the fear of being grateful for the fear. People talk to me and I don't always understand them. They speak a language that sometimes frightens me. Of one thing I am sure. Behind every fear they make me live, there is always a question postponed and an answer to understand. And it is they who come to throw themselves in my face so that I decide to return once more to life. To mine. Of course.

I like our complicit silence after love. I like the warmth of your body resting on the right side of mine. I like to feel the damp warmth of your inner thighs against my tired leg. I like to ruffle your hair with my fingers that are still unsteady from pulling out deafened moans and cries in the middle of the night. I like looking at your breasts in repose and guessing the design of my lips when I kissed them just now. I like to close my eyes and listen to your still irregular breathing. I like repeating your name in a low voice and feeling your smile without seeing it. I like to tell you that I like you. I like to hear you laugh softly before telling me that you like me too. This is changing life. It's living everything you feel like living. You and me. You and me. And nobody else. In secret. Away from the world.

In my life I need someone who does not like me, who speaks ill of what I say and do, who criticises me without knowing me, who cannot stand me or see me, who wants to be better than me, who challenges me, who insults me. Life manifests itself more intensely in the communion of its opposites. If I only had in my life those who loved or praised me, who valued and excused me, who accepted me without doubting me even a little, I would not be who I am today. I need those who wish me harm, as they need me. They are the ones who allow me to respect myself even more. I am the one who gives them through me the possibility to change. The perfect symbiosis. The necessary coexistence. Life at its best.

Men are generally more needy than women. It may seem like a contradiction, but the truth is that men show it in an unclear way that confuses those who don't know them. Men's neediness is revealed in the attacks they make on women. Every needy man attacks some woman, in whatever form. Neediness takes power away from men. It makes them feel diminished. It makes them invent reasons to attack the person who causes them this feeling of diminishment, this painful difficulty in asserting themselves. Neediness is the poison of many men. That's why they prefer football, porn films and beer. They don't feel so fragile. They can more easily attack women from a distance and think they come out unscathed. Without guilt. As if they had scored the winning goal in the last minute of the game.

I no longer want anything to end. I prefer everything to change, to transform, to challenge me, to disturb me, to leave me breathless. What ends, generally leaves no trace or history. What ends, ceases to be what perhaps never was or was for such a short time that it ended without leaving me with a tear in the corner of my eye. Ending is above all when it is no longer worth continuing. To finish is to understand that something is already over before it's even finished. The truth is that in my life I prefer everything to be transformed, because transformation is the antithesis of repetition. Everything that repeats itself in the same way, without anything different each time, could be my way of not facing my fears. But my fears always have a short shelf life. I like to face them still fresh and never spoiled by use and tiredness. It is the only habit I allow myself. Like a prayer following a nightmare. It's as simple as that.

I've thought about dying and smiled. I've thought about living and smiled. I've thought about you and smiled. I've thought about nothing and I smiled. Whatever I do, I smile. I'm a smile. Nothing more. Just a smile. A smile that makes me feel good about myself. At ease with my silence and my scream.

A man in love is often a man lost between the need to appear secure and the emotional and rational babble that reigns inside his heart and head. For many men, being in love is a plague, a fucked-up spell to manage. They prefer just to like, because those who like don't suffer nor are afraid of losing. In fact, men are afraid of being cheated on. That's why they are almost never affectionate for more than the initial period of passion. That's why they rarely give themselves away. They prefer to live on the surface of emotions and feelings, on the edge of pain, in the distance of the I love you feeling. They make themselves strong, but tremble. They seek out their male friends to remind themselves where they come from and where they really belong. They laugh with them and have a few drinks to stop believing in the nothingness of the very little they have. They prefer to live this way. They cling to shit that has no smell, to fires that they don't feed, to problems without solution, to addictions without salt, only to justify what they don't want to know the justification for. Many men in love are cowards. They are afraid of love. They are afraid of suffering for love. They prefer addictions of silent pain.

I am no longer afraid of failing, because I have understood that I never fail. The truth is that I stopped demanding anything of myself. I stopped allowing myself to be demanded. When I don't demand of myself, I don't fail. I just do what I do in my own time. To demand something of myself is to go against my nature. It is forcing me to be who I am not. I stopped demanding a long time ago. Instead, I started doing only what I am passionate about, what makes me smile and feel alive. On the contrary, I have started to get those who demand me out of my life, because those who demand me don't respect me. They have only interest.

I am a story, a soul and a life. I was born with emotion at the surface of my skin. I grew up in fear of who I was told I was. I died for once before truly beginning to live. I built a path without thinking much about it. I just wanted to be happy. As I am today. Someone who has long ago stopped doing and having in order to be. Someone who does and has only because he already is.

Some people get annoyed with me when I say that I can do whatever I want and say whatever I feel like. Something in me makes them pretend to want to prove me wrong. I believe they have not yet realised that it is not my behaviour that irritates them, but their lack of attitude that makes them exasperated. Nothing I do is new to the world. Many people do the same as me. The point is that they don't understand that I like to provoke them to do the same, to live their lives to the full. If they just stay at the point of judging and criticising me, they will always excuse themselves for what should be unapologetic. If they decide to feel what I provoke them to, nothing else will be the same in their existence. Everything in them will start to heal without leaving any more visible marks.

Feeling is the best way to live. I particularly like to find myself in feeling. Everything is different from when I think. To feel is to choose to receive a kiss of love from myself. To feel is to go beyond what I fear to know about myself. It's flying without ever having tried my wings. It is to miss who I am not yet. It is to love whom I know it will be possible to love. It is being able to smile without fear of crying with joy. It is to see what is not visible with the naked eye, lens or microscope. It is learning to let go without thinking of coming back. It is to free myself from everyone and make my light shine. Not to die alone. Rather to live without fear of my company.

What I can do is not always enough for me. There are times when I need to go further, to take a step further than usual, to follow a path never dreamed of or recognised. I don't think too much, because I know that thinking too much makes me hesitate every time, and to hypothesize about giving up and not following my heart. My whole life exists in the name of my desires and passions. Even in the worst of times, I am sure of what I choose, just because I choose without thinking about outcomes or conclusions, predictions or analysis, horoscopes or futurism. I know that the best for me always comes wrapped in the most beautiful smile in my heart. The one I give only to myself. And to those I love. And to no one else.

I always choose for myself, for the smile I bring to my heart. I always choose for who I am, for the light that I feel growing in my chest. My choices have my strength. They have my energy. Making them makes me feel free, and freedom is a choice that is mine alone. When I choose to smile, I receive with a smile. I always want to choose in a way that puts colour in my days. Meaning. I don't want to forget where I came from. I don't want to forget who I chose to come to be. I will always want to be an angel seduced by the colour of your wings.

There are things that belong to me, but which I also know are not mine. I don't give up what I feel, but I know that everything fits only in a moment. If I believe I'll feel the same way forever, I'll waste the magic of the moment. I have always needed the conquest of every second. Patterns bore me. Rules kill me. I have no patience for those who complain about constant not-so-good phases or routines. The unexpected is part of me like a forever love. Discovery is my favourite poem to read whenever I want more life. I don't waste time with those serious conversations someone thinks they should have with me. I prefer smiles and laughter and a good glass of wine or a nice cold beer. Some people, think I'm irresponsible, a guy who never left his teenage years. They can think what they like. I am convinced that they would like to live my way. Or to have the courage to say everything they think. And what you feel. As part of something meaningful. With life. That's all.

As crazy as it may sound, sometimes I am sure of who I was in other pasts. I usually feel it when I meet someone who was somehow part of one of those experiences. Not infrequently, however, I also feel it when I visit a place or watch a film or documentary on television. They are not illusions, not even hallucinations, because there are times when I really perceive smells and sensations as familiar as those I am experiencing today. I believe that I am a primary sum of all my lives, a fusion of ghosts, loves and fears of all that I have lived and been prevented from living. I am certain that I am within me a mixture of who I was and who I am supposed to be. In the middle, right in the middle, is what I lack to fill. I don't know what it is, but I don't want to know it either. I think I'd get bored knowing the ending. By all means.

Denying has never done me any good, or any good at all. Lying to myself has always brought me only reasons to keep running away from the same thing. Apologising for everything and for nothing only helped me to do the same and each time nothing new. I needed to stop in order to continue my life without inventing any more disguises and deceit. It hurt more than touching an open wound. It stirred things worse than the greatest of fears. It took my breath away with the force of a punch to the stomach. It knocked me to the ground like the attack of an enemy too strong for my lack of grace. The truth is, I needed to fall to get up. It was essential to stop doing what others expected me to do in order to value myself. It was necessary to write and sing my own song, even if no one wanted to hear me anymore. It was wonderful to make my life into a summary of so many words.

If I can no longer avoid crying, I no longer do anything to stop it either. I like to perceive myself crying, faithful to my sadness, to the hours that pass like seconds in the search for a meaning for what seems to have no meaning at all. When I try to wipe my eyes it is as if I want to erase words I can no longer hear, words repeated too often, in my ear and against my chest, like prayers without faith. There is little left for me but to cry until I have no more tears or air. I know that when I get there, I'll invent new words to raise my eyes and sketch a faint smile. I've learned that to cry is to want to understand what you're running away from. However, I have cried for departures and also for arrivals. And even for absences. As if crying was also smiling.

I find it difficult to believe in a love that sleeps. I believe more in something that you wish was love but didn't become it. A body without desire may not mean an absence of love, but someone who makes excuses for not being able to love the one who loves them the way they should might as well be a lack of love. One of the things that distinguishes us from animals is our ability to feign love. No animal shows love without actually liking it. We people lie and cheat in the name of what we dare to call love. Perhaps we should observe animals more in their dealings with love. I believe we would have a chance to bring out in ourselves what we often call pathetic or too ridiculous. The truth is that we seem to forget that love is never reduced to our space alone. It is not short-lived. It travels beyond itself.

The love I attract is a reflection of how I respect myself. You may say the opposite or even criticise what I stand for, but life shows that the love I receive is identical to the love I feel for myself. I have had times in my life when I believed I was being good to others and attracted a violent and disrespectful love. It took me a while to understand that although I was kind to others, I was not kind to myself. I disrespected myself in my intimacy with myself, in my silence and my solitude, in the way I tortured myself with thoughts and emptied myself to give myself to others. My exterior is the faithful image of my interior, even though I may want to convince myself otherwise with complaining and tears. Nothing is different unless it is changed first. What I think creates what I think. What I believe defines me. If the will to change me is weak, sooner or later I stop attracting love and convince myself that I am the son of a lesser god, one of those gods without a kingdom that promises without ever giving anything.

Every now and then, I need to close my eyes and let everything go its way without me. There are times when I allow too much to be demanded of me. It only lasts a short time, but long enough to leave me feeling like I haven't been consistent with who I am and who I want to continue to be. The truth is that I try to understand why I tolerated what I shouldn't have tolerated and I always come to the conclusion that I still have old ghosts that mess up my determination and my path from time to time. They are thoughts and episodes that I thought were lost in the years and in the labyrinths of my memory, but which in the end never disappeared at all. It is in these moments that I understand the importance of always being conscious. It's at times like these that I understand how easy it is to enter and never be able to get out of places with no name or life.

I have a spirit that is capable of crying. It always does so in silence so as not to disquiet me. I know it does it because I feel it sobbing very tenuously inside me. Its crying always happens when I'm sad. I stopped insisting that it stop, because it doesn't listen to me, at least not until it feels me smile. I have a spirit capable of crying. Deep down, it's like me. It cries because it wants to be cured of love. It is not afraid of the pain it feels, or even of what it feels. It is only afraid that it will stay there forever, even after it is healed.

When I don't know what I'm going to do tomorrow, I feel privileged. The truth is that I can choose anything, from doing nothing to doing everything I've never done. For me, not having anything to do tomorrow is having every chance in the world open to me. I can catch the first train and get off at any station I feel like, laugh all day at nothing and everything at the same time, bake a chocolate cake or walk barefoot through the streets of my city, watch a movie in the cinema or just the sea, stay all day in bed or help those who need help, play with children or talk to other people, start writing a book or paint a picture, listen to music or be silent, swim or surf, live or die. When I don't know what I am going to do tomorrow, I can imagine, and when I imagine, I smile, and it is in smiling that everything gives me more pleasure to be done.

I no longer live slowly or quickly. I anticipate life by a millisecond. The time of a smile before everything. The instant in which I transform life for myself. The moment when I choose what no one else chooses. That is all. My life before life. My life without futurisms or tarot, without a crystal ball or predictions. My life mine. Only mine. No one else's.

Happiness came to me from the moment I started to feel my smile more. I began to experience things to learn something and others because I learned something. I understood that life has paths that I only discover when I forget the logic of what I already know. I ran away from that which insists on running away from me. I got up to let go of those who want to make me fall. I stopped asking for what I like and started liking what comes to me. I killed the importance of time with a slap of my freedom. I became a good son-of-a-bitch for myself, because I don't want to be a son-of-a-bitch for anyone. I realised that I am happy because I have people in my life whom I love and don't see as mine. I want from them only the most beautiful smile they can make me smile.

Each person who crosses my path has a soul that is somehow connected to mine. Some touch me more, not because they are more important, but because we have stories in common to take up again or simply to decipher. Each soul has an eternity that is its own and another that exists in its communion with life. Mine is becoming lighter and lighter. Other souls approach it more easily, make it smile, speak to its heart. I have always loved souls who have a heart, because they are less afraid. They are more courageous in speaking of themselves. They love without asking to be loved. They kiss my lips without wanting to destroy my kiss. They see a side of me that without them I wouldn't even know it exists. They are souls without the desire to be more than souls.

I have stopped making any kind of promise to anyone. A promise is also an obligation and I refuse to feel obligated to do anything. A promise is also a certification of a trust that I don't need to ask anyone for. I no longer tolerate on my side those who do not trust me. I do not promise anything to anyone because I do not control anything. My choices often make me change direction and a promise forces me to stay behind. I always choose not to promise anything and to surprise. I believe that everything that happens to me naturally has more to do with me. I don't know how to live any other way. I don't know forced truths or uncompromising lies. What I have known are unfulfilled promises and wounds without scars that are very difficult to heal.

I remember you to survive your absence. I love you because the essential thing is to love you, even if you don't feel the same way about me. My body trembles at the imagination of your touch, at the idea of your kiss. I feel you in me without ever having touched you. My reality is made of what exists only in my heart. My happiness lies in knowing that you are a part of my life. Whether you like it or not. Whether you know it or not. You are mine. My dream lives in a time that is mine alone and has become as big as that which is not yet part of me.

No matter how many nights I go without sleep, there will be one when I finally close my eyes and go back to sleep. No matter how much pain I endure, there will be one that finally doesn't stop me from smiling. No matter how many lies I tell, there will be one that I won't be able to tell without lowering my eyes. No matter how many excuses I find, there will be one that even I won't be able to convince myself of. No matter how many crazy things I do, there will be one that one day will seem too crazy. No matter how many silences I seek, there will be one that will finally make me long for the sound of your voice. No matter how many loves I experience, there will be one that one day will seem like a reunion with myself, a story of just one story, a hand glued to my heart.

Every now and then I like to go up to my heaven. I sit on a cloud and my god comes to me. Usually I go up there because I want to cry without anyone seeing me. I am not ashamed. I just feel like doing it alone. My god doesn't count. It is me in large size. His hand rests on my shoulder while I cry. That's all. He says nothing unless I ask him something or look in his direction. Sometimes my father and brother join us and the four of us cry without saying anything. Crying is our language. If I have to cry, let it be with them, because the return is always happier after crying in my heaven.

In life, there are no limits except for those who travel with a map and a time to arrive. The freedom to be able to choose roads, airports and train stations to leave and live, gives sanctity to the journeys and grace to the arrivals. I am a fearless traveller, an adventurer in my own light. One day, I will want to leave without a destination and return date. I will put on a backpack, a compass in my heart and leave everything and everyone behind. Don't get me wrong. The truth is that sometimes we must be reborn away from everyone. I believe that those who are not prepared to be born again, are not prepared to die, nor to live.

I was not made to run without stopping. I abhor rushing and breathlessness. I don't seem to know what I'm doing here. One would say that I want to command time or subject it to what it is no longer supposed to be. The truth is that I like to feel each thing in its own moment. Palpating it. To breathe it. Calm it in me. Deserve it. I'm more the slow but sure type than the rushed and careless type. I place a lot of importance on details, but I don't obsess over their order or temporality. In fact, I easily accept changes and limitations. I just don't accept withdrawals and disrespect. They make me angry. They make me really want to yell at my god, whoever he wants to be with me.

Sex and intimacy are not the same thing. Sex without intimacy is just fucking. They say that once in a while it's also good to fuck, especially because it makes us realise the importance of intimacy. Only intimacy makes you want to stay beyond the moment, to embrace more than just their body, to say what you've never said before, to hide time under the sheets, to stare at the ceiling and smile silently as you stroke the hair of the one sleeping on your chest. I love sex with intimacy. I don't know how to do it any other way. Only intimacy makes me giddy, exuberant, generous, fierce, fiery, adventurous, creative, tender. Only intimacy makes my skin shiver without being cold.

I can't stop looking at you. You are in front of me and I am not able to take my eyes away from yours. Your silence is my wound. I know that I have done you wrong, but don't stay without saying anything to me. Your silence is the certainty that I didn't know how to speak to you in other silences. I won't tell you that I did wrong, because that would be like forcing you to look down. I don't want that. I only want you to let me look at you until you feel me once more as you felt me before. I don't want to promise you anything. You know I'm not one for promises. I just want you to let me look at you and recognize in my eyes the love I've always felt for you. It's still there. It's always been in the same place, close to my heart, close to your soul. Maybe that's why I can't stop looking at you. Maybe that's why I hope this silence will end in a kiss. In the urgency of understanding and being able to continue looking at you without fear of your silence.

I'm not looking for stardom. I just want to have fun. I don't yearn for print runs of thousands of books. I just want the joy of writing about what I feel and believe. I don't need crowded lectures. I just want to communicate my truth to whoever feels like listening to it. I am not looking for anyone's approval. Mine is enough. I do not look for love. I feel it in the simplest things I come across every day. I don't look for anything. I have everything I need. I have eternity with me.

Sometimes I love being stupid, because for me a stupid person is someone who doesn't give a shit Shout who thinks they're smarter than he is. I've had the opportunity to do that several times. It's hilarious to consciously give power to those who want it. It's magical to find out what people are capable of to keep it. Being stupid on demand is a blessing. It allows me to learn even more about the stupidity of others.

I always feel happy when I do what I should have done, say what I should have said, think what I should have thought. I feel happy because when I do it I am me, I am myself, without disguises or lies. Nothing gives me more pleasure than living my life as an adventure. In fact, it is an adventure. The adventure of going out and always coming back inside myself, without ever wanting to stay outside for long. I am someone who feels who they are without fear of what they feel. Inside me there is a light that is only mine. A light made of truth and joy. When I feel it and let myself be guided by it, I choose me over everything else, all those for whom I previously gave up being who I am. I am not abandoning or disrespecting them. Quite the contrary. I am enabling them to make a choice identical to mine. That is all. Nothing more.

Recognising someone you've never seen is as strange as accepting what you don't believe in. The connection that we have with all the people that we meet down here always manifests itself in a very particular way, but there are some who carry eternity written in their eyes and a smile that kisses us without touching. We begin to miss them the moment we see them again. They seem to have everything and don't need to sacrifice anything of what was always theirs. They tattoo us from the beginning, without saying it, because they don't need words to talk about what they already carry with them. They are ours without ever ceasing to be so.

They come to remind us of who we were back then, in a time forgotten by time, not as if we were nobody, but as if we could go back to being whoever we want. The truth is that they provoke the desire to feel wanted again. Alive. Both. In a promise without swearing. In a desire achieved before even being lived.

I always loved my father, but I feared his unhappiness very much, because it took away his patience and made him often irascible or indifferent towards me. At home, he was always a very quiet man. Quiet in his questions and answers. I remember him almost always reading, sitting on his leather sofa, immersed in a thick cloud of smoke from the cigarettes he smoked almost without a break. There were times when I surprised him with his eyes fixed on the ceiling, far, far away from his living room, perhaps in the place where he would like to have the courage to leave. Sometimes it was in his office that I caught him, his gaze resting on the end of his cigarette, in silence, again probably building dreams and stories he never got to live. When he looked at me, he didn't seem to see me, at least not the way I liked him to see me. He would shake his head slightly as if to ask me what I wanted. I would give him a timid hand signal and leave him alone with his thoughts. I have always loved my father, but I wish I had known where he would like to go. Maybe he would invite me to go with him.

Life dies a little more in me every time I run away from a passion, every time I fear to leave the uncertain, every time I listen and believe those who tell me about wisdom, fear and shame to justify not risking, every time I refuse a trip, in the times when I don't believe in my dreams, in the moments when I diminish myself by what they say about me, in the time when I let myself stay too long in dissatisfaction and fear, in all the doubts I put on the choices of my heart. Today, I refuse to live that way and live life by the second. The preciousness of each instant makes me not want to waste it anymore. That is the reason why I live each moment of my life not as if it were the only one, but as if it were the one in which each time I am appeased with who I am not yet, but who I am on the way to becoming.

I like to be where I know I should be. I like to know that I don't have to go anywhere else. I like to feel that life is mine and nobody else's. I like to realize that I choose only what has to do with me. I no longer look for my freedom outside myself. I no longer go anywhere to be free. I no longer make concessions to who I am. I am happy because I treat freedom on a first-name basis. I am happy because I know how to be happy.

Life is a blessing. It breaks the rules. Dare to love without fear. Have fun without measure. Take responsibility without fearing responsibility. Run risks. Laugh a lot. Follow your impulses. Dream big. Do what you are passionate about. Change for love of yourself. Live where you like. Stay only where you feel like staying. And never listen to those who tell you otherwise, because they are always the ones who would love for you to be like them.

I love to invent crazy things without being out of love. What is wonderful does not necessarily have to be loved. I remember things that somehow became unforgettable in my life without being for love. I remember divine drunkenness in the nights when I was a disc jockey without knowing how I managed to be one. I have memories of moonlit nights on the beach dunes, lying on my back, talking to myself and counting the stars so as not to fall asleep. I no longer forget my teenage outbursts of fear written in the form of poems that I read solemnly to my totally stoned friends. I remember the great fashion falls from which I emerged miraculously unscathed and laughing in a stupid mixture of relief and senselessness. To tell the truth, I found in each of these crazy things the adventure of not wanting to find answers, but just having fun. Love, that one, was postponed in time, not out of fear, but because at the time pain still had no place in my heart.

Everything that happens to me helps me to identify what I feel. Absolutely everything that happens to me helps me to be aware of the emotions that are running through my chest. Everything that happens to me is done so that I respect myself even more and can change what disrespects me or makes me suffer. To accept feeling is to allow myself to live what is for me. Everything I have done up to now results in what I am living now. If I don't like it, I must change the way I live that very thing. Only in this way can I prepare myself to receive the truth of all that is for me and has been kept away. When I get everything that is supposed to be in my life to be in it, I will live the calmness proper to those who only do what has to be done.

I always separate my personal life from my professional life. I avoid every time that they depend on each other. I am the same person in both, only different in my silence. Alone, I keep quiet to think and smile in the gratitude of being able to live the way I do. In a consultation, I do not speak to make room for listening. My work is largely the art of knowing how to listen to and feel those who come to me. I never give solutions. I provoke emotions. I create hypotheses. I make people smile. I talk about dreams. I listen to stories. Actually, maybe there isn't a big difference between my two lives. Maybe they're both the same. Or not. I don't know. I just know that the only thing that can somehow make them similar to each other is perhaps the fact that they are made of the same passion. Maybe. I don't know. I don't care either. The truth is that I like both of them enough to be able to keep them apart, although very close inside my little heart of a poet and dreamer.

A relationship is built a lot on longing. The idea of not being with the person we would like to be with now preserves the feeling. Pain seems to be always present where love is felt. It is an almost stupid duality, but it is undoubtedly one of the conditions for the preservation of harmony. Opposites attract, but the truth is that they cannot destroy themselves. Too much longing leads to a lack without measure. Too much pain makes one want to forget the feeling. Constant absences tend not to remember the person who is no longer needed. There are no great formulas. There is only trial and error. There is learning. And there is the beauty of the quick longing and the expected reunion, which always seems so little and is so much.

Teach me once again to dream. Please remind me how to do it. Time has made me forget the colour of my dreams. I lost them between who I was and who I am not yet. Teach me to dream. I became afraid of not having them again. I need your courage and your smile, your strength for me to see them once again in myself. I no longer know how to dream. Life took them from me without asking me if I wanted to give them up. Or was it me who ignored them for fear of not achieving them. Teach me once more to dream. Please remind me how to do it. Don't leave me without dreams. I'm nobody anymore if I don't dream again. Please teach me once more to dream. I don't want to live without dreams. I don't want to walk arm in arm with the sadness of not being able to dream.

I can only remove from my life what I accept as mine. As long as I deny its existence or fight against it, I will never be able to remove it from me. To accept it is to let it belong to me that which I wish did not belong to me. If it is with me, it is because it is mine, it is part of what I need to live without fear for it to definitely leave me. I only stop fearing what I accept to live. I only give up wanting to feel it again after understanding its meaning in my life. The most important things are always the ones I can release after suffering at its hands. Everything is lighter without its presence. Everything finally goes its own way, no longer by mistake or through suffering. Only in the name of my freedom.

I don't believe in people who don't respect me. I have no doubt that nothing that comes from them will ever be of any help or benefit to me. As a kid, I learned from my father to be suspicious. With age, I have learned to be cautious instead. This way, I suffer far fewer disappointments and can more easily escape from such people before their poison enters my veins and makes me say or do something foolish that I will surely regret. Over time I have realised that in some cases indifference can also be therapeutic.

I like to help those who want to help themselves. I don't lift a finger for those who don't want me to. I don't allow myself to be with those who want to deceive me so that they can continue to deceive themselves. I no longer let myself be easily surprised. I no longer let myself be carried away by false sorrows and scattered joys. I like to look deep into the eyes of the people who come to me and feel what they are really feeling and don't want to translate it into words for me. I am not always very equal in my methods, but I am always a thoroughbred professional. I don't give up on those who don't want to give up on themselves. I tear my skin off for them. I die on the watch if I have to. Just because that's who I am. The sum of everything I feel and believe.

I never miss what I didn't do. Not even what I'm yet to do. I have no urgency for anything. I'm not in a hurry to get anywhere. Novelty fascinates me, but I don't look for it. It comes naturally in my life because of my attitude towards the old and worn-out. I can no longer dedicate my time to that which does not bring me anything new or gives me more of the same. Not all people understand me, but I also don't care if they understand me or not. I've reached a point where I've stopped feeling compassion for those who don't feel it for others. I don't care anymore about these theories that if I'm not good, life will take its toll on me. What I decided a long time ago was to respect who I am and who others are, without that implying being such a fool as to allow them to disrespect me. I am worth more than that. I deserve different. Life thanks me. I know that. I feel it in what it gives me every day. It gives me a unique meaning for all that I take in and repudiate. It fills me with joy and peace.

At this moment when almost nobody cares to understand why they are here, I make a difference. I want more and more to activate my sensitivity to understand and locate myself. If I feel fear, I move forward. If they want to stop me, I draw my sword and do not retreat. Nothing is the same in my life when I don't give up on myself. Everything receives my smile. Everything takes my touch. Everything becomes part of myself. Everything makes me believe that to understand myself is to provoke my limits and fall in love with my talents. Amen.

I can now accept my two ex-wives in peace. Each in their own time revealed in me what I needed to understand of what I had not yet understood about who I was not yet being. In their own way they helped me grow in self-respect. What I thought I lost with them turned out to be a reflection of what I gained. I respect them for what I felt in their own time for each one, for the children they gave me, for the moments that made us get what we have today. I am no longer the same. I couldn't. The way I see myself today is an extension of what I couldn't be and live with them. It could only be that way. I hope they think the same. I really, really do.

Sometimes I still wonder why I am only attracted to what is different, to what nobody else wants or seeks. It seems that there is an invisible magnet that leads me to the strangest places and the people who are most different from me, even if they are similar in some way. I always approach the most difficult, that which makes me want to get it. I find it difficult to accept the easy. I always believe that it is short-lived and will not interest me for long. I like that which makes me feel what I have never felt before, that which I feared too much and for no reason. I can't stand sameness and lack of passion, schedules and precepts. It seems as if a voice is secretly telling me to flee from them like the devil flees from the cross. It's not a matter of fear. It's my own matter. Only mine. It's part of my centaur side. Of my planet Venus stuck in the house of Scorpio. Bold, like this. Like me, with me.

I have an immature side that manifests itself only in my maturity. I don't know how to be just someone more or less. I need my immaturity to be more than I need to be. I want to be who I haven't been yet to get to where I never thought I'd get to. Being immature gives me the courage I need to dare to face all the fear that makes me an orphan of life. I love to set aside prudence and reasonableness and live in a way that only I know. It is my rebellious side and adverse to deposits of irony and lies. I want to burst into laughter and redraw all my dreams. The time has come to be immature once again. Tonight, I set off on a new, long journey to happiness. This time, with no turning back.

I have lived arm in arm with the pain of living without understanding why everything had to happen as it was happening. Not knowing my truth made me believe lies for too long. Grief competed with me for a front seat. Fortunately, I sank and fell into depression. I fell so I could rest. I let myself stay on the floor so I could breathe again without pain. I got up slowly, a little each day, until I could sit up and look out through one of the windows of my house. It was a time of heroics and giant steps over the weakness of barely making it. One day, I smiled again and realised that it had all been worth it. I understood that every pain has a story and every story has a reason for its pain. Mine had to do with respect. With the lack of respect for me.

I'd like to read your palm and discover my name written on the lifeline. I'd like to lift my eyes and realise you have yours closed as you listen to my reading. I wish I could touch your hair and tell you a future that was ours. I find it difficult to speak to you of things that I do not wish to see through the terraces and the lines of your hands. I fear that you will see me only as the one who tells you about presents and possible tomorrows. I wish you were not indifferent to the way I hold your fingers and run the palm of my hand with my trembling finger. I wish that the smell of your perfume gave me the courage to tell you things that only my heart knows. Maybe you would pull your hand from mine and leave. Maybe you would never come back. Maybe you would have hated me. But I would have told you of my love. I would have told you how unnecessary it is to forget what I feel. Not as if nothing was, but as if everything could still be.

When you celebrate fifty-five, the conversation is more or less the same as when you turn thirty. Not before. The twenties have something of an irresponsibility and still very long life to live. After thirty, things change perspective a bit. Suddenly, it is easier to say that you are already this or that age and you accompany these words with a look of strangeness and almost fear. From the age of forty and fifty onwards, most of it loses its grace and becomes too serious and tasteless. It seems that age is proportional to the stupidity of not being able to do and say some things. One gains notoriety, position, money, and joy gives way to the ridicule of having and wanting to follow too many rules and norms. Wrinkles and baldness become symbols of maturity and false emotional stability. But not for me. I did just the opposite. Turning forty was the best gift life could have given me. It was the moment I freed myself from approvals and obligations. I grew my hair long, I put on bracelets again, I changed my clothes and I got a tattoo because I felt the same desire as someone who decides to marry the love of his or her youth. It was at the age of forty that I followed my dream of being free, without bosses or orders, in the desire to help myself by helping others. Twice I ran out of money. Twice I raised my head and stood on my side. I returned to my road, the one that has ditches and slopes, chasms and bad weather, but also the one that makes me smile every day as if the sun were always beating down on my face. After fifty, I discovered the madness of being happy with me, without fear of loneliness, without fear of showing my sensitivity, without time for those who want to take away my dating time with myself. Today, I am passionate about my life and I don't cling to anything. I know that everything passes and I want to live each moment as if my story could depend on it. I turn fifty-five. I have never felt so young. I have never felt so free. I have here a place that is exclusively mine.

I am good because I am good for me. I am no more this or less that than anyone else. I am incomparable, and whoever does not understand what I mean by these words does not understand what I am doing here. Whoever compares themselves to me loses the best of themselves. Tell me to fuck off if you want, but don't say "fuck off" to what I make you feel. What you feel when you look at me, the anger, the injustice, the insecurity, the frustration, the love, the fear, is nothing that I have to give you, but what you need to work on yourself. Shit on me, because I am nobody compared to you. You are special to you and you don't need anything more than what I am making you feel. If it hurts, go inside. If it scares you, face it and understand. If it makes you angry, stop and feel what your chest is telling you. I am nobody to you, but I can make you look inside by the simple fact of existing. You will do the same to others. And others will do the same to others. That's the way life works. You don't always get what you want, but you always get what you need. Cheers.

There is a direct link between what I say and what I believe. I am no longer able to smile if I don't feel like it. I can no longer waste time on things that have nothing to do with me. I no longer talk about what does not arouse any interest or passion in me. I don't change my opinion if what I hear or am told makes no sense to me. I have long understood that my life is the result of the choices I make. If I choose with fear, I suffer. If I decide without fear, I live. It's my life and I do with it what I want. Fuck the others. Let them live theirs. I hope they do well, because I like to know that there are happy people here and there.

I do not waste a single day of my life. I know that each one of them is being offered to me so that I can make a difference. I take advantage of it because it is by making the most of each day that I show I accept that everything only lasts as long as it has to last and leaves the mark that it has to leave. I take advantage of each day, not as if it were the first or the last, but as if it was unrepeatable. I enjoy each day, but without wanting to make it the key to my happiness, because that lies in my attitude. Each moment is magical, if I can see and feel its magic. Each instant is a challenge for me to live what comes next. Each minute can be worth an incarnation as long as I am consciously grateful to be living it. I receive what each one has to give me and I don't run away from feeling what I am feeling when I receive it. I already understand that heaven toasts on my behalf each time I choose to face something rather than endure it.

In a relationship, trust is not the purpose, but simply the assumption. Lack of trust hurts, even when it has no reason to. It is a wound without a bandage. A time without breath. A defence without strategy. If there is no trust, there is fear. If I live in fear, I move away from my path. And I don't want that. If it hurts, I want to know why it hurts. I need to look the truth right between the eyes. I need to be at peace. Whoever is with me owes me that, otherwise I leave. I immediately know that the search is elsewhere, on another horizon. A long time ago I stopped being afraid of the unknown. I packed my bag and left. I return home. I lie down on the sofa and let myself fall asleep. There is no one like me. I'm sure of it.

Joy is not in things, but in the way I feel them. There are things that don't touch me and others that are part of who I am. The ones that don't mean anything to me stay with me for a short time. I give them away. I share them. I throw them away. I only keep the ones that have to do with me, the ones I feel like they are wishes and promises to be fulfilled somewhere on my journey. Everything I choose also chooses me. Of that I have no doubt. We are like lovers of more than one life. Souls connected by timeless and inexplicable bonds. Things that I don't want to know where they come from, nor where they go. Things that bring me joy. That's all.

My life has strength. So I don't go against it. I do not force it. I do not question it. I do not rationalise it. I do not control it. I don't worry. I let myself go. Without thinking. Just feeling. Choosing what I feel is for me. Talking about what I believe in. To provoke with my truth. Celebrating. To smile. To live without fear. Watching everything stay in its place. As if it was magic. As if it was a gift. For me.

If I believe, I do. If I don't doubt what I feel, I live. Even without understanding. Even without questioning the reasons or asking for clarification. Like a wave on the beach. Like an open door to a garden. In a very own way of being in life. Unique. Only mine. Without words. Just listening to my heartbeat in peace at last. At last without fear. Ready to receive you.

My courage helps me to understand the unpredictable. I am no longer afraid of almost anything. I am free and everything is justified in my freedom. Everything is in the right place. Life flows. Heaven and earth come together to bless me. You too, though you don't know it yet. When you do, you will be like me. Master of your destiny. Master of yourself.

I have a nameless passion for all my madnesses. I am a collector of only those whose logic is lost on stage, especially right after the beginning of the first act of the play. I have a great difficulty in being an actor to those who ask me if I am crazy. My madness is genuine. It's mine and it's different from all the other people I know. It has that I don't know how much seriousness that distinguishes it from the rest. It is a healthy madness. A madness proper to those who love life. Of those who don't mind being treated like a madman.

I like to look at a photograph and find out who is in the background, sometimes even half out of focus. I do the same with my clients. I like to understand what moves them, what is behind their smiles or tears. What they are still hiding from me. What they still don't know. Their more lateral side. Their deepest centre. The little things that make them resist. Or run away. Or suffer. Or make me like being this way. A mixture of provocation and sensitivity. A passion that puts me in their place. Makes me feel like them. Makes me be themselves without ceasing to be myself. In the magic of helping them to smile. A little more every day. Until they fly again without me. Without anyone else. In freedom.

Fear comes and goes. There is a natural balance in my relationship with it. Some days I feel it awake and wanting to fight me. Other days, I don't even remember its existence. I believe I wouldn't be who I am if I decided to run away from it every time. I have long accepted it as part of the life I have chosen. The important thing is not to give it too much importance. The talent is in understanding in it only what you are supposed to understand. I know it's a warning. A sign. A question mark. A door to the unknown I seek. That's the reason I don't have to do much to understand why I'm feeling it. All I have to do is return to my road. I follow it without giving a rope to fear. Turn it into caution, without recognising in it what it never was. Not being afraid of feeling fear. That is all and only that. To transform this life into the life I really want to live.

I no longer believe in that god that some priests still speak to me about. I have no room in my life for ignorance and for those who foment fear. Even today, when they speak a little more openly of their love, they end with an inevitable prose of punishments and sins. I have had enough of the multi-faceted interpretation of the bible and the twists and turns of texts lost in time. My god is joy. It is sharing. It is that voice that tells me what it knows is best for me, that tells me to dare to be happy and not to listen so much to the pessimists and those who claim to be the bearers of their truth. My god tells me to smile a lot, that forgiveness is bullshit to make me feel guilty of something I am not, that rules are to be questioned and majorities are almost never right. My god asks me to leave behind those who want to fuck up my life, who betray me and lie to me, who envy me and plot, who speak ill of me behind my back and steal from me every day. My god is my friend, so he is my god.

I don't care about explanations for what makes me smile. I am from a world where you like those who celebrate life, in whatever way. I want to share my joy with you. My world. Come. Bring curiosity. Nothing more. The rest is up to me. Pick your heart up off the floor and open it halfway. Take the canapes of smiles and the toasts of happiness and place them inside. Close it again and feel. Be collectors of hugs, little mountains of kisses, crosswords of love. Make life worth living. My world is for those who believe in the power of a word, in the perfection of the imperfect, in the flight of the stork, in the silence of noise. Here, everything is allowed as long as the hostages are happy and the battles are fake. In my world, the importance lies in the encounter and not so much in the memory of the encounter. Here, one lives in the now. Yesterday is forgettable. Tomorrow is some shit that doesn't exist yet.

I like it when my soul gets full of life, when it seems to leave me and come back even more crazy with life. I like it when it tells me I have to go to Venice or just stay at home, when it makes me forget the time and forbids me to wear a watch. I am ecstatic when it makes me feel in love with someone and teaches me that nothing is worth a lie. The way we relate to each other is more like two jobless dancers mocking hunger than two masons carving a story together. The truth is, I'd be lying if I said my soul doesn't make me laugh. Quite the opposite. Something about it tickles both my boldness to be a writer and the madness to be its accomplice. Or better. In the eagerness to be its lover.

I started to succeed when I started not thinking about him. Or rather, when I started to understand it in a way that made much more sense to me. I understood that success exists from the moment I like myself and what I do. In reality, success is not a matter of luck, but of choices. It is what I came here naturally to do. It is what makes me live in passion, it is what I love and allow to accompany me on my path. Success is who I am. In my freedom to be.

You do not want to live up to their ridiculous expectations of you. They ask you every day to be who you don't want to be, to do what you don't want to do, to think like them and stop thinking for yourself. Do not allow your desires to be limited. Do not submit to what you fear. Raise your eyes and dare to defend your point of view. Without fear. Or even with fear. Fuck it. Make yourself count. You deserve to live a meaningful life. You deserve your freedom. Your daily smile. Don't just be a shithead who complains about what you keep allowing. Tell the person who messes with you every day to fuck off. Don't believe that there's nothing else beyond that mediocre little life of yours. There is much more. Much more. You just need to dare to believe in yourself and realise that others need you more than they need themselves. Without you, they are nothing. Without you, they die. Without you, everything is different, because you count for more than they do. Put your foot down. Say no. Slam the door and go find what is made for you. Your passion. The reason why you are here and not somewhere else. Life goes with you. That's all you need to know.

I need to forgive myself for what I didn't do. I need to understand why I chose not to. The truth is that I am detached by nature. Maybe that was the reason. Forgiveness does not assist me as if I was a hotel receptionist. Quite the opposite. It turns its back on me. If I don't call it, it ignores me. It's an animal without habits. A liberal in a dictatorship. I have to want it on my side to give me some of its attention. Forgiveness is not the same as listening to someone or tipping them. It is much more complicated. It's an attitude of wanting without hesitation, of understanding without having to lower your eyes, of laughing without fear of showing your teeth. To forgive myself for what I have not done, I first have to accept what I have done. Simple. But capable of making me question everything.

I enjoy meeting people who I seem to know from another life or history. I feel that an unknown part of me reveals itself at the same time. I recognise a smile, eyes, a gesture, a senseless feeling that captivates me immediately. There are times when I see myself as a knight I don't know where and other times when I am travelling on a slave ship on the way to a new continent. I know I have to fit in, but I can't. I stand still and smile. Suddenly I am far away, yet very close. I speak without understanding myself. I listen without understanding. I laugh and cry without finding the reasons to do so. Something new has once again entered inside me. I feel as if I am being invited to watch my own life. It is strange, but it does not frighten me. I've experienced it somewhere in time. I've felt it before. It's mine. It always has been.

I no longer think as I used to. I no longer say the same things I used to say. I no longer do anything that bothers me or disrespects me. Before, I allowed things that today I understand are no longer necessary. Maybe they were never necessary. Maybe they were allowed before. Yes. I was like that once. Permissive and wanting everyone to like me. I was exhausted, without the strength even to smile. I wanted so much to be liked that I stopped being myself. I complicated even the simplest things. I felt unhappy without understanding the reason for my unhappiness. I branded myself with a hot iron and it took a long time before I could smile with my eyes. But it happened, and I never allowed myself to be different again.

I no longer feel like I'm dying every day. I have found a direction, a path that I know is mine. At least today. Tomorrow, I don't know. The truth is that I have stopped worrying about tomorrow. I live today what I want to live and what I don't even know I am living, what I do without thinking or feeling, what I repeat. I live and I love to live. I chose to live instead of dying in life. I decided to smile instead of being indifferent. I chose to see my path give me another way. Life. My life. Enough that I no longer feel like I'm dying every day.

Inside my heart, everything finally makes sense. What happens to me is in harmony with what I believe. Nothing that I feel is different from the truth that I recognise as being mine. I became who I am because I stopped believing in what was expected of me. I listen to myself more now than ever before. I have understood that I live intensely when I am grateful for even what hurts or makes me suffer. Living intensely is this. It's looking at who caused me pain and understanding that it was a lesson. It's not running away from all my emotions. It is to open one's heart. It is not being afraid. It is not wanting anything. It is to stop complaining about what I have and don't have. It is to understand that if there are shadows around me it is because something is preventing the light from reaching me. Nothing more.

I have no patience for people who are neat and tidy. I believe that behind that immaculate order there is always chaos about to burst. I look at them and I can almost predict what they stop saying and doing. However, I am sure that they cannot erase from their minds the constant thoughts of fear and the desire to shout at the sky for not giving them the necessary courage to break with all this regularity. I see in them what maybe even they can't see. I see in them a life being extinguished. I see in them a hope transformed into illness. I see in them intolerance towards themselves.

I know your embrace is still available, despite everything I did to you. I lied to you with truths you didn't want to hear. I kissed you without thinking that you would never forget my kisses. I made you mine without letting me be yours. I hurt you with words of silence. I made you feel loved when in truth I don't even really know what love is. I promised you to be honest, I was and I hurt you. I disappointed you with who I said I was. You're right to wish me ill. I didn't change to please you.

What moves me is joy. I love smiling and laughing, drinking a good drink, listening to music and sneaking into parties. I like to surprise those who respect me and to be surprised by those who like me. I love the sea, the beach, the waves, the sand and the sun. I love the rain, the wind, the thunderstorms, the puddles and the fallen leaves. I love long dinners with those who make me smile. I like conversations in front of a lit fireplace, sitting on the floor, my back against the sofa and a good red wine served in just one glass for both of us. I am crazy about a good cheese. I like to play the guitar for myself. I love making love in the least expected places. I'm a fan of poetry and freedom of expression. I love what I do and even what I don't do yet, but know that one day I will. Period. The truth is that sometimes I feel like a grasshopper. I need to jump much more than to fly. Jumping also takes me far, farther than I sometimes dared to believe.

Sometimes nothing else matters. Suddenly, everything has more than one solution. From one moment to the next, you realise that you are happy in your happiness and you smile, because your smile is what best defines you. Not even your eyes. Not even your hands. Happiness is in your smile. Only in your smile and nowhere else.

I no longer feel guilty about anything. What I did, I did. I can no longer change anything. I got the good habit of accepting what can no longer be differently. To live is also to accept the past. To live is also to be happy for what I can do from now on. I no longer believe in constraints. I believe in choices. I believe that living can be the most genuine of improvisations. I believe that I am prepared to see both sides of many more things. And that doesn't come from age. It comes from wanting to have more fun while I'm around.

Stop complaining about everything you allow. Change jobs if you don't like it and they don't value you. Give your relationship a shake-up if it has become meaningless and insipid. Change your look if you get tired or bored. Do what you have been meaning to do for so long. Don't put it off any longer. Find ways, not excuses. Find strategies, not escapes. Don't allow yourself to stay where you no longer want to stay. Don't give in to your fears and go after your dreams. It is your life. Don't let others keep running it.

Every day, I challenge myself to be honest with myself, to speak my truth without fear of being ridiculed or criticised, to tell off those who disrespect me or make me suffer, to be who I have always dreamed of being, to be myself. I believe in myself. I believe in what makes my heart beat. I believe in daring to hold my head up high and choose what I know is about me. I believe that I can live without fear of anything and with nothing to be afraid of.

I like what stays and only sometimes what goes away. I always have trouble dealing with indecision and lies. I need company and loneliness in different proportions. I need to find myself in the midst of all the people living around me. I don't have emotions with contraindications or allergies. I feel them all as part of me and live them all with the same intensity. There are times when I tremble with fear and other times when I laugh with joy like a clown, but I believe that this is the only way I can live without fear of living.

I remember as a kid waking up to the sound of Frank Sinatra's voice or Glenn Miller's orchestra. My Sunday mornings would start in a way that was never different and always gave me a strange feeling of both safety and intrusion. I remember I would get dressed and go into the living room, where my father was sitting on the couch reading and listening to music. He would lift his eyes in my direction and then lower them as if to tell me to leave him alone. Something in his selfishness fascinated me. Something in his attitude endeared me. The truth is that I identified immensely with that man, although I did not understand him until close to his death. I don't know if it was because our blood was the same or if it was because our souls were one, but I was extremely proud to be his son. I always felt it. Maybe he didn't. Or he preferred never to say he knew, not even before he died. We were at peace. That's enough for me.

I like new beginnings, new perspectives and new realities, births and unplanned things, roads I've never travelled that take me to places I've never been. I like to live what I have never lived, of uncompromising and detachment, of smiling faces and sincere looks, of feeling time as if it was not time and distance as if it was an easy mathematical formula to solve. I like you when you don't demand anything from me, when you take me in without asking for justification, when you turn your bed into my bed, when you satiate your desire in my desire, when you let me fall asleep in silence after love. I like to go back on my way as if it was a new beginning, to smile in my freedom and the absence of constraints and expectations, to know that I am like this because I don't want to be any other way. I am here. That's all I need to know to start something new.

Every dream has a time. After that, it becomes a mistake. I can try to make it come true, but its time has passed. I can insist to achieve it, but nothing is as it was when it was still possible. Every dream has a time and when I don't realize that it is so, I lose the opportunity to feel what new dreams I have in me. The old dreams hide the new ones from me. They mask them with unimportant thoughts. They take away their own time.

I don't want to live in need, but in awareness of what I lack. Neediness makes me expect to receive from others what I lack. Awareness makes me seek within myself what I feel I need. I begin to understand a little more about love, not in the forms that are most sought after, but in the ways that are least seen. What I lack rarely matches what others have to give me. It is an illusion created so that I believe I am equal to others. The truth is that my faults only hurt me when I see them as they are not or when I give them too much importance. Otherwise, they are like words spoken in the ear by those who know and understand me.

Most of us tolerate too much disrespect and others' superiority complex. We are afraid to look each other in the eye and stand up for ourselves. We are afraid of embarrassment, mistreatment and bad manners. We often shut up in front of a doctor, an engineer or the head of whatever for fear of retaliation or humiliation. I no longer play these games. I know my rights and my duties. Anything that goes beyond those limits is subject to my tolerance, which is very small. I am neither angry nor frustrated but I do not tolerate arrogance or injustice. I am my own man. I don't want to be anybody else's master.

I am enjoying more and more the feeling of not needing to worry. Worry makes no sense from my perspective on life. Most of my worries have always been a waste of time and energy. What I do know is that I no longer worry about predictions or futuristics. I live each situation according to its moment. The possible and the impossible no longer bother me. Solutions are worth what they are worth. The important thing is the time I no longer waste on anything that does not deserve my time. I live each thing for what it asks of me while it happens. I no longer want to control anything. I give myself to life because I am part of it. I don't have answers, but I don't worry about the questions anymore either. I accept what is, and change what no longer makes sense. I stopped being afraid of fear and of others. I started to take responsibility in a natural way for what I create, and I started to live with a smile on my face. That is all.

My great challenge is to do for myself what I never thought I could do for others. Everything that before seemed to have some sense loses all its meaning. I have understood that I don't need anyone, not even those I believe I need. If I do, I depend, and I find it difficult to depend, even if only for hours. I want to disconnect from everyone without being alone. I want to be with others without ceasing to be with me. I want to fall in love without passion destroying me. I want to be yours without ceasing to be mine. I want to live without ever allowing myself to be made to forget that it is in freedom that I found the path to the life I chose to live.

I always find it difficult to understand and accept when someone tells someone to love themselves. One cannot love oneself without understanding love. Nowadays, the idea of what love is is for the most part very confusing. Nobody knows anymore the distinction between loving and liking, between wanting and being, between fear and indifference, between bastard and son of a bitch. They believe they feel when in fact they just need. Need is perfidious, because it is often confused with love. It punishes without mercy. It kills without taking life. I believe that for someone to love themselves, they must first respect themselves. Only after respecting themselves will they be able to begin to understand themselves. And only those who understand themselves, come to love themselves, because you only really love those who understand themselves.

The most important things are not those I want, but always those I receive. If I attract violence it is because I need to know how to deal with it, not by becoming violent, but by learning to turn it into a classroom for me. It is not always easy. I have a natural tendency to react when I should just act. I have never been a middle ground person. For me, things either are or they aren't. I have no patience for moderation or excessive pondering. I have always been more adept at seeing to feel, going to live. If I have to lose or die, I always do it with a smile on my lips. I don't know how to be any other way. I don't want to be any other way.

I wouldn't be who I am without my intuition. I believed in what I felt, without anyone else believing. I risked madness for the sake of even greater madness. I dared to wait for me where no one knew my name. I chose what few others would choose. I went forward without praying or asking for opinions. I continued on my way without doubting the direction to take. I felt what I had never felt it was possible to feel. I managed to reach where my heart asked me to reach. I gave meaning to what had no meaning. I finally became capable of being myself.

The more I feel alive, the less death frightens me. I am irritated by the idea that we should fear what we don't know. The greatest joys of my life have been unexpected for me. I did not know them more than death itself, and yet I loved to have received them. The continuation of life no longer worries me. I am here and I want to make this occasion the best of all. When I die, I will be able to see what I don't know. Who knows, maybe it really is paradise.

I reversed all my priorities and became different. I let sensitivity and insanity mingle so that people could understand me better, but not really. Sometimes I get the feeling they won't understand me until after I'm dead. Fuck it. It's not important to me. The relevance is in what I feel and make myself feel and never in the triumph of my opinion.

My whole life changed from the moment I realised my value. It was a huge breakthrough when I understood that I was capable of being good to myself without harming anyone. Going against everything I had been taught had a strange taste of mutiny. I never quite understood this whole business of looking after others before myself, of loving others without others respecting me, of helping others without also helping myself. There are assumptions that we accept without questioning. I like to imagine myself living without them. I love confronting them and doing whatever I feel like doing. I have realised that I am only good to myself when I don't give a damn what they think and say about me.

Death made me question about the true meaning of life. I am told of so many theories, possibilities, energies, frequencies, beliefs, that I decided to think without thinking about any of it. I wanted to understand where I position myself in the middle of all this. I realised that none of this makes more sense to me than what I still don't know. I believe that if it gives me pleasure and makes me feel good, it is because I am being me, regardless of the energy I emanate, the frequency I am on, what I believe in. I think we all think too much, are too influenced by too much of what we hear, and don't stop to feel ourselves. I want to stay where I feel good, where I understand it makes sense for me to be. From here, everything happens and uncomplicates itself. My truth is in the way I feel. My passion is in what makes me smile with my eyes. My life is in my joy of being joyful.

There are days when I don't feel like going to bed. I feel like prolonging the night until there's nothing left but a huge scream of tiredness in my body. Even so, I stubbornly leave it almost without breathing until I finally climb to the first floor to lie on the bed. My light-hungry eyes scan the darkness for a point of balance. My legs ache and my shoulders tense. Before, I didn't know what was wrong with me. Today, I know I'm missing even more than your absence.

I don't want to lose my ability to laugh. Reality has moments when it bores me. It makes me bored. It makes everyone bored. I no longer have the patience to live reality without laughing. One would say that everything seems unfunny or not understood. It seems that nothing makes sense beyond the meaning they want to assign to it. I know I could be wrong, but there are times when I want reality to go to hell. I need to laugh to keep believing. Reality without laughter has become the fate of the unfortunate.

9 798885 713639